忍びの術

The Shinobi Scroll
of the Wolf

Samuel Franco

1

The Shinobi Scroll of the Wolf
Written by Samuel Franco
Edited by Fernan Vargas
Copyright © 2025 Fernan Vargas

First Printing: 2025
Off the Books, Books
Chicago, Illinois USA 60107

DISCLAIMER NOTICE

The authors and publishers of this manual accept no liability whatsoever for any injuries to persons or property resulting from applications or adoption of any of these procedures, considerations or tactics presented or implied in this text. This publication is to be used for reference only, and its content is not designed or intended to function as a self-teaching manual. No part of this book may be reproduced in any form or by any means without permission, in writing from the publishers or the authors.

TABLE OF CONTENTS

Prologue   Pg. 7

The Invisible Pack   Pg. 11

Circles of Trust   Pg. 17

The Territory Mindset   Pg. 23

The Nomad Code   Pg. 29

Cold Camp Discipline   Pg. 35

The Watch Turn   Pg. 41

Rituals Beneath the Pines   Pg. 47

The Sentient Perimeter   Pg. 53

The Language of the Eyes   Pg. 61

Leading From Behind   Pg. 67

The Lone Watcher   Pg. 75

Ghost Signals   Pg. 81

Adaptive Packs   Pg. 89

The Refuge Principle   Pg. 95

The Returnless Scout   Pg. 99

Death for the Living   Pg. 105

The Packless Phase   Pg. 111

Burden of Loyalty   Pg. 117

When the Pack Fractures   Pg. 123

The Doctrine of Distance   Pg. 129

Wolves Within Walls   Pg. 137

Long Winter Readiness   Pg. 143

When the Alpha is Silent   Pg. 149

Legacy Without Insignia   Pg. 157

Appendices   Pg. 163

忍びの術

PROLOGUE:

The Quiet Fang

The Wolf Scroll begins in silence, because silence is where the shinobi lives. Not in legend or light, but in motionless watchfulness beneath frozen boughs, in footsteps that vanish behind them, in loyalty that needs no return. The Quiet Fang is not just a principle—it is the beginning of all others. It is the unspoken oath that binds the pack before the first word is ever exchanged, before territory is marked, and long before the mission is named.

This doctrine is not built on hierarchy or conquest. It is shaped by cold camps, shifting ground, and bonds forged without chains. The wolf-shinobi does not protect what he owns, but what he has chosen. Territory is not possession— it is responsibility. And the pack is not blood—it is trust, tested over distance, hardened through hardship, and refined in silence.

To follow the Wolf Scroll is to walk a path of enduring vigilance. It is to rotate through the night watch when sleep is scarce, to guard those who do not know your name, to move without signal, and to lead without taking credit. It is to live as a nomad, yet belong more deeply than the rooted.

It is to feel the threat before it shows itself, and to be gone before the danger strikes—leaving only peace behind.

This scroll is not a manual for warriors seeking glory. It is a doctrine for those who protect from the shadows, who defend without ownership, and who give without recognition. The Quiet Fang is their first discipline—sharp, silent, and ever ready. It is the beginning of the way of the nomadic guardian.

忍びの術

Samuel Franco

CHAPTER 1:

The Invisible Pack – Kinship Without Chains

There is no ceremony to joining the invisible pack. No sigils to wear, no binding rituals, no vows spoken beneath full moons. For the shinobi who lives by the Wolf Scroll, kinship is neither assigned nor claimed—it is recognized, moment by moment, action by action. The invisible pack is formed not through lineage, loyalty pledges, or mutual ideology, but through the quiet alignment of instincts between those who walk similar paths through silence and threat.

The bond begins when two warriors recognize each other not by name, but by presence. The shared glance during a patrol, the mutual nod before entering uncertain terrain, the wordless exchange of supplies in bitter cold—all of these are threads, and with time, they weave a fabric stronger than any contract. Trust is not demanded. It is observed in motion: how one chooses to carry their burden, how they watch your back without being asked, how they react when everything goes wrong and nothing can be gained from staying.

To the outside world, this pack may seem fractured or even imaginary. There are no ranks, no councils, no declared allegiance. The wolf-shinobi moves alone when needed, disappears for long stretches, and may not even speak to their own kind for weeks. But when they reappear, the bond remains unbroken. Because the invisible pack is not maintained by presence—it is maintained by principle. Each member lives according to the same code, regardless of where they are. And that code carries more weight than proximity.

Kinship without chains is not a rejection of closeness—it is a refinement of it. In the old world, loyalty was often mistaken for ownership. Armies demanded obedience, families demanded sacrifice, and leaders demanded submission. But the invisible pack makes no such demands. It offers a different kind of belonging—one where respect is earned, not assumed, and freedom is not the absence of commitment, but the foundation of it. Each wolf chooses to stay, not because they are forced, but because they know someone else would do the same.

In this kind of pack, every bond is practical. Trust must translate into action—into shared firewood, overlapping fields of vision, a hand on your shoulder at the exact moment your knees begin to fail. You do not owe your life to the pack, but you offer it because theirs has been offered to you. It is never spoken aloud. That kind of language is unnecessary when the stakes are elemental. Cold. Hunger.

Silence. The mission. The pack. You endure for each other because you've already seen what each other can endure.

The invisible pack allows for difference. Members may be quiet or loud, fast or methodical, soft-eyed or hard-faced. What unites them is not personality, but purpose. Not sameness, but synchronization. Even among wolves, temperaments vary—but what binds them is their reaction to threat, their rhythm in movement, their understanding of territory. For the shinobi, this rhythm is developed through lived danger. You learn who will move when you move, who will stay when you stay. That knowledge is earned in the field, not in training halls. And when it is earned, it requires no reaffirmation.

There is a discipline to remaining part of an invisible pack. It means checking in without being asked. It means rotating watch even when tired. It means staying gone when presence would compromise the mission. It means accepting that, sometimes, your only reward is that someone else gets to wake up safe. And it means being ready to walk away the moment your presence puts the others in danger—because the pack comes before the self.

And yet, paradoxically, it is in this willingness to leave that the deepest bond is formed. The invisible pack is one of mutual autonomy. It refuses to imprison its members in obligation or proximity. Instead, it trusts that each will return when the time is right, when the terrain calls them back together. And when they do, there is no guilt for the time apart. No resentment. Only the nod, the shared glance, the seamless return to watch rotation and meal rationing. No explanations are needed. They were never required.

Sometimes, the most vital members of the pack are never seen. The advance scout who clears the path days in advance. The rear guard who stays behind to intercept a pursuing threat. The sentry who never comes off rotation because they know the rest are nearing collapse. These are the silent threads holding the pack together. They may be mistaken for loners, even outcasts. But within the invisible pack, their presence is felt deeply—even in their absence.

What makes this kind of kinship so resilient is its adaptability. It survives terrain, time, and trauma. Because it is not based on ritual, it cannot be broken by distance. Because it is not based on command, it cannot be fractured by disagreement. The invisible pack holds not because of pressure, but because of understanding. And when the world changes—and it always does—the pack changes with it. Members shift, fade, return. But the bond persists.

To be part of the invisible pack is to carry others within you, always. You move alone, yet you move as a part of something larger. You sleep, knowing someone else is awake. You fight, knowing your strength comes not just from your own body, but from the knowledge that you are never truly alone.

There is no flag for this pack. No motto. No uniform. Only a shared discipline, a rhythm of trust, and the quiet certainty that, somewhere in the cold, someone else is walking the same path.

CHAPTER 2:

Circles of Trust – How Warriors Choose Each Other

Trust, in the world of the shinobi wolf, is not built in a straight line. It spirals—slow, deliberate, and often invisible to the untrained eye. It does not begin with introductions or affirmations. It begins with observation: how someone steps, how they breathe under pressure, how they respond to the unknown. In the pack, trust is not something you declare. It is something that emerges, slowly, like the moon behind shifting clouds.

The circle is the natural shape of trust—closed but flexible, defensive without being restrictive. In every unit, patrol, or improvised alliance, the warrior must discern who belongs in which circle. There is the outer ring: acquaintances, allies of the moment, those who can share fire and information but not secrets or burdens. Within that, the trusted: those who you would bleed beside. And at the innermost ring, few are ever admitted—those for whom you would take the burden of failure, even if it costs you everything.

Warriors do not choose each other with sentiment. They choose each other through shared endurance. It is in how you respond to discomfort, to failure, to long nights of silence under falling snow. No one earns trust through charm or rank. They earn it when they have every reason to abandon you—and don't. They earn it when they hold the line even after the mission is compromised. When they return from a scout without needing to say, "I saw it through." You already know they did. That is the weight of silent reliability.

In the early phases, trust is a test neither party admits is happening. The shinobi watches how you carry your pack. Whether you ration fairly. Whether you keep watch at your appointed hour, or let fatigue override duty. They look for your response when plans fail. Do you complain, blame, collapse—or adapt? The ones who make it into the inner circle are not the strongest or the fastest. They are the ones who remain calm in chaos and generous in scarcity.

And yet, the wolf-shinobi does not seek to build one perfect circle and seal it forever. The terrain changes. Missions rotate. People fall, wander, return. Trust must remain fluid. The true warrior does not cling to familiarity at the cost of effectiveness. They know when to let go of an old bond that no longer fits the current terrain—and when to allow someone new in. The ego must be left behind. There is no space for nostalgia in a mission zone. Only functionality, rhythm, and the invisible language of earned belief.

When two warriors trust each other fully, words become optional. One lifts a hand and the other moves without hesitation. This telepathy is not born—it is forged through countless moments of accuracy under stress. It is not about knowing each other's thoughts, but knowing each other's instincts. That kind of trust cannot be simulated. It must be lived.

Yet this kind of closeness is dangerous if given too easily. The wolf is cautious for a reason. Betrayal, whether through intention or incompetence, can cost lives. That is why circles of trust are layered. The outer rings are not to be disrespected. They serve their purpose. You can move with people you do not fully trust—as long as you know where they stand. What causes failure is not a lack of trust, but a failure to *calibrate* it.

Every warrior must become a quiet strategist in human judgment. Who can you trust to finish a mission under fire? Who can you trust to keep a secret under capture? Who can be trusted with decisions, and who must be given only tasks? These assessments must be made without ego, without wishful thinking. You must trust what is shown, not what is promised.

Circles of trust are also built on reciprocity. To be trusted, you must *be* trustworthy. It is not enough to expect others to hold your back. You must hold theirs first, with no guarantee of return. You show up when it's not your turn. You carry more than your share. You remain silent when speaking would protect your reputation but endanger the mission. Every choice writes a line in your ledger—and others are watching, even if they say nothing.

And so it becomes a slow dance of investment. Small risks, taken over time. Quiet gestures. A shared meal. A coordinated exit from a compromised zone. The hand that steadies a brother's knee during a long march. The moment you offer your coat without being asked. These small choices accumulate until one day, without fanfare, you're in. And one day, without warning, someone else is in with you.

There is no formal notice. No one tells you, "You're trusted now." Instead, someone places their life in your hands without hesitation. Someone sleeps while you watch. Someone follows your signal in a blind corner. That is your confirmation. Not praise—trust.

But this closeness, this shared bond, is not permanent. It must be maintained. Trust is not a fortress—it is a trail. It must be walked, often, and reinforced. Neglect it, and it fades. Abuse it, and it breaks. The shinobi understands that the strongest pack is not the one with the deepest history, but the one with the most active discipline.

Lastly, warriors must know when to *shrink* the circle. Not all bonds serve the mission. Loyalty is not blindness. Sometimes those closest to you falter—and you must have the strength to adjust. To reposition them in your map of trust, without cruelty, but with clarity. Because the mission comes first. And if the bond endangers the pack, it must be reshaped, or severed.

To choose another warrior is to offer them a portion of your safety, your silence, your success. And to be chosen is to carry that same weight in return. In the world of the wolf-shinobi, nothing is more sacred than being inside someone's trusted circle. And nothing is more dangerous than misjudging it.

Choose wisely. Watch carefully. And once the circle forms—guard it with your life.

CHAPTER 3:

The Territory Mindset – Defending What Isn't Yours

In the code of the shinobi wolf, territory is not possession. It is responsibility. The distinction is critical—and it separates those who dominate from those who protect. The wolf-shinobi does not claim land, people, or power. They inhabit spaces temporarily, observe their flows, and defend them as if they were their own, all the while knowing they never truly are. This mindset—defending what isn't yours—is both a burden and a discipline. It requires humility, vigilance, and restraint.

A wolf in the wild knows its range, but it also knows that nothing within it belongs to it. The trees are not its trees. The prey is not its prey. The territory is defined only by the tracks left behind, the trails scouted, the hours spent watching from unseen vantage points. The shinobi moves the same way—unseen, unthanked, and often unknown. They protect villages they were not born in. They safeguard people who will never learn their names. They maintain balance in places that may one day forget they ever existed.

This principle separates the guardian from the conqueror. To defend something without owning it requires a unique kind of discipline. Ownership tempts ego. It invites control, attachment, even entitlement. But the shinobi must remain unattached—not emotionally numb, but free from possessiveness. They must guard homes as if they were their own, while always remembering that they are not. Their authority comes not from power, but from presence. From observation, endurance, and quiet action.

The territory mindset demands observation first. Before a shinobi can defend, they must understand. This means walking the perimeter not just with eyes open, but with senses tuned to the unseen. Every slope, every gust of wind, every rhythm of life in a given place must be studied until the terrain itself becomes a silent ally. To defend is not just to intercept a threat—it is to know when a threat is coming long before it appears. It is to feel the change in silence. The subtle shift in temperature. The missing birdcall. The echo that doesn't quite match.

This kind of understanding cannot be rushed. The shinobi may spend days or weeks in silent reconnaissance, learning how a village breathes, where it aches, what it fears. They listen without intrusion. They remain unseen until the time to act arrives. When it does, they move with precision—not to claim the space, but to restore it. Their fight is not for conquest. It is for continuity.

There is a kind of pride that emerges from defending what is not yours—but it is not the pride of ownership. It is the pride of stewardship. Of knowing that someone will sleep more peacefully because of your watch. Of understanding that your efforts, while unnoticed, made someone else's world safer. And then, when the threat has passed, walking away without asking for thanks. Leaving no mark but the continued peace.

The territory mindset also teaches adaptability. No two terrains are the same. A desert village requires a different eye than a coastal one. An urban street demands different timing than a mountain pass. The shinobi must blend into each environment, learning its language and rhythm, adjusting their methods without losing their core discipline. Just as a wolf adapts its hunting to the shape of the land, the guardian adjusts their protection to the contours of the threat.

Defending what isn't yours also sharpens the sense of boundaries. The shinobi must know not only where to act, but where not to. Interference, even well-meaning, can become intrusion. The guardian walks a tight line between help and disruption. They do not impose their way. They align with the natural flow of the place, inserting themselves only where necessary—and then only with precision. They do not change a system to feel important. They preserve it, even if it would have failed without them.

There is loneliness in this way. To protect without belonging, to guard without being invited, can be an isolating discipline. But the shinobi accepts this as part of the path. They know the value of what they do is not determined by recognition. It is determined by results. When the child wakes and does not fear the night, when the villagers sleep through what could have been danger, the guardian's purpose is fulfilled—whether or not their name is remembered.

And yet, this mindset is not without tension. There will be times when the shinobi feels drawn to a place. When a bond forms. When the territory starts to feel like home. This is when the discipline is tested most. The line between guardian and settler must be guarded carefully. Attachment, once it hardens into possession, can dull the senses. The shinobi must remain light-footed, emotionally agile, prepared to leave when the time comes—because one day, it will.

Ultimately, the territory mindset is about service. It is about choosing to step into danger on behalf of others, even when those others don't know you're there. It is about protecting paths you don't walk, homes you don't sleep in, and lives you'll never touch directly. It is a way of seeing the world not as something to take, but as something to preserve.

To live by this code is to accept that your work will often be invisible. That your sacrifices may never be acknowledged. But the shinobi wolf does not need applause. The land itself bears witness. The wind carries wordless thanks. And somewhere, beyond your watch post, a child laughs without fear—because the shadows are quiet tonight.

That is enough.

CHAPTER 4:

The Nomad Code – Belonging While Always Moving

To be a nomad is not simply to wander—it is to carry your sense of place within you, even when the world offers you none. For the shinobi who follows the Wolf Scroll, movement is constant, but it is never aimless. Each step serves a purpose. Each journey, though quiet and unrecorded, is part of a larger pattern. The Nomad Code is not about escape or detachment. It is about learning how to belong without settling, how to connect deeply without becoming rooted, and how to serve without being seen as permanent.

The world tells us that belonging requires stability. That to have purpose, one must remain in a single place, become part of its rhythm, its history, its soil. But the shinobi wolf knows otherwise. Belonging, in this doctrine, is not tied to ground. It is tied to intention. To vigilance. To quiet acts of service that do not require ownership. A true guardian is defined not by where they are from, but by what they are willing to protect—even if they must move on before the gratitude ever catches up.

The Nomad Code teaches presence without permanence. When the shinobi arrives in a new place—be it a village, a ravine, a crumbling outpost—they do not announce themselves. They do not seek titles, positions, or roles. Instead, they observe. They blend. They study the currents of tension, the cracks in the rhythm, the subtle signs of imbalance. They align themselves with the flow of the place, not as conquerors or caretakers, but as temporary stewards. While others take root, the shinobi becomes the wind between the trees—always moving, but never lost.

To live this way is to accept a certain kind of solitude. You will not be celebrated. You will not be missed when you leave. At times, you may even be suspected. But this solitude is not the same as loneliness. It is chosen. And within it lies the power to connect with all places, without being trapped by any. The nomadic guardian does not belong to the land—but they serve it as if they do. Their loyalty is not to borders, but to balance. Not to flags, but to lives.

The strength of the Nomad Code is in its detachment—but this detachment is not indifference. It is a clarity that allows the shinobi to make decisions without bias, to see a threat without the distortion of personal interest. Because they are not invested in territory for gain, their presence can be trusted. Because they will not stay long, their interference is measured. And because they know they will leave, their actions are precise and meaningful—every gesture, every defense, every word, weighed carefully.

Some may view this as weakness—an unwillingness to commit, a fear of being known. But that is a misreading. The Nomad Code is not about fear. It is about clarity. When a shinobi chooses to stay, even temporarily, it is never out of comfort. It is a decision made from duty. They belong where they are most needed—not where they are most welcomed. They do not chase warmth. They go where the cold is deepest. And when the balance is restored, they leave, quietly, even if their heart would rather stay.

To master the Nomad Code is to learn the art of invisible roots. The connections you form may not be visible, but they are no less real. A child who grows up unafraid because you cleared a threat they never saw. A village that forgets to be anxious because your presence, though unspoken, shifted the tension. These are roots that do not tether you, but still bind you to something greater. You will always belong to the places you've protected—even if they never remember your name.

Movement itself becomes ritual. Campsites are broken with precision. Tracks are erased. The land is left better than it was found. Even in absence, the shinobi is a presence. The wind remembers their steps. The earth holds their discipline. The people, though unaware, carry the peace they left behind. This is belonging not through ownership, but through contribution. Not through presence, but through impact.

The Nomad Code also demands internal stability. When the outside world offers no consistency, the shinobi must cultivate it within. Rituals become anchors: how you sharpen your blade, how you prepare your food, how you take your watch. These small acts become your home. They remind you who you are, even when everything else is unfamiliar. They give shape to the endless path. Discipline becomes identity. Stillness within movement.

There will be times when the temptation to stay is strong. A place where you are finally seen. A voice that asks you to remain. A cause that could use more of your time. But the Nomad Code whispers: *You were not meant to stay.* You were meant to pass through, to shift the balance, and then disappear like morning frost. This is not abandonment—it is alignment. Your value is not in your presence, but in your purpose. And when that purpose is fulfilled, lingering can only dilute it.

There is also a deeper reason for the code: vulnerability. The more you stay, the more you are known. And the more you are known, the easier you are to target. A shinobi is not only a guardian, but also a keeper of silence. Movement protects not just them, but the mission. Their nomadism is a form of armor—a cloak that makes them hard to trace, hard to predict, and harder still to capture.

And yet, even in motion, there is community. Other nomads will cross your path. You will share fires, trade stories without names, offer food without keeping score. These moments, brief and wordless, create a different kind of belonging. A brotherhood of movement. A sisterhood of silence. A pack that spans continents—not through constant contact, but through shared purpose.

The Nomad Code is not a rejection of belonging. It is its evolution. It teaches that you can belong to the world by refusing to be owned by it. That you can find connection not in staying, but in serving. That you can carry your identity like a blade—sharp, useful, and always close, no matter where you go.

To belong while always moving is not a contradiction. It is the highest discipline of the wolf-shinobi. And when done right, your path may disappear behind you—but the peace you leave in your wake will remain long after you're gone.

CHAPTER 5:

Cold Camp Discipline – Endurance Over Comfort

The cold camp is not just a location—it is a philosophy. It is the space between survival and surrender, the quiet place where warriors decide what kind of guardian they will be. To the shinobi wolf, the cold camp is a proving ground. There is no fire to soften the wind, no shelter to dull the ache. There is only discipline. And it is in this discomfort that the nomadic guardian learns their true edge—not how hard they can strike, but how long they can endure.

Comfort is the enemy of readiness. The more one seeks warmth, the more vulnerable one becomes to what lies in the dark beyond it. Firelight draws attention. Excess invites dependence. A shinobi in the cold camp does not reject comfort because they enjoy suffering—they reject it because every unnecessary indulgence threatens the mission, dulls the senses, and exposes the pack. Endurance is not glorified pain; it is strategic clarity. When the world turns hostile, it is not the strongest who survive—it is the most prepared.

Discipline in a cold camp is expressed in small, consistent acts. How the sleeping mat is placed—not for softness, but for concealment. How rations are consumed—not for satisfaction, but for sustainability. How one moves in the early hours—not groaning, not complaining, but rising with quiet efficiency, boots laced, blade checked, breath controlled. These rituals shape the mind as much as they maintain the body. They sharpen the will. And in the cold, will is everything.

To remain in discipline when no one is watching—that is the mark of a true shinobi. Cold camp life offers no applause. There is no reward for staying alert when others sleep, for eating less so others may eat more, for resting in silence when exhaustion pulls at your bones. But these are the decisions that form the soul of the guardian. When the weather turns bitter, and your only warmth is your breath, your posture, and your principles—then, and only then, do you find what you're truly made of.

This form of endurance is not brute resistance. It is quiet adaptation. The shinobi doesn't fight the cold—they move with it. They breathe slower. They sleep in layers, not for comfort but for containment. They pack light, but with purpose—every item carried is earned, every tool serves a role. They learn to embrace stillness, to extract warmth from posture, from shared body heat, from strategic movement. They do not waste energy resenting the elements. They conserve it by flowing with them.

Cold camp discipline also teaches emotional regulation. The environment tests not just muscle, but mindset. The irritability of prolonged discomfort. The anxiety that arises from vulnerability. The longing for fire, for food, for home. These are natural feelings—but the disciplined warrior does not allow them to dominate. The shinobi acknowledges the emotion, then breathes past it. They prioritize function. They control their reactions not by suppression, but by presence.

The cold camp is often where leadership is revealed. Not through commands, but through consistency. Who rises first? Who checks the perimeter? Who gives up warmth so the weakest can rest longer? Who volunteers for the far watch when the wind cuts deepest? In the absence of formal rank, discipline becomes the hierarchy. Respect forms around reliability. The one who endures quietly becomes the one others lean toward in moments of doubt.

Endurance also binds the pack. When each member commits to the discomfort—without seeking comfort at the cost of another—the bond deepens. Shared suffering, faced with shared discipline, creates a kind of trust that no oath can match. No one complains, not because they are numb, but because they all know the stakes. In this silence, a different kind of language emerges. One that says, *We are in this together. I will not fail you.*

Still, the discipline must be internalized—not enforced. A shinobi cannot be policed into resilience. They must believe in the purpose behind the pain. Cold camp discipline is a choice repeated every night: to stay quiet when your limbs tremble, to go on watch when your body cries for sleep, to choose rations that keep you alert rather than full. These choices, layered over time, become character. And that character, more than any weapon, is what carries a guardian through prolonged adversity.

In times of extended deployment—what the doctrine calls "long winter readiness"—the cold camp becomes not a place of transition, but a way of life. The shinobi must settle into it without ever growing soft within it. There is danger in adaptation too—when a warrior grows too used to survival mode, they can lose sight of mission, of people, of cause. Cold discipline is not about self-obsession. It is about clarity, about remembering what you serve, even when all the world is reduced to cold breath and tired hands.

There are moments, rare and fleeting, when warmth finds its way into the cold camp. A second ration shared. A dry patch of ground beneath pine canopy. A moment of stillness with someone who understands without speaking. These are not indulgences—they are reminders. The shinobi does not reject all comfort—they simply do not rely on it. And when such moments arise, they are treated with gratitude, not expectation.

Leaving the cold camp is its own discipline. When the time comes to move, the shinobi packs swiftly. They erase their tracks, scatter their ashes, leave the land as untouched as possible. The goal is invisibility, not legacy. The memory of the camp belongs to the land, not to the one who slept in it. And as the shinobi continues the mission, they carry with them the lessons of endurance: that comfort is temporary, but character is lasting.

The wolf-shinobi does not seek hardship—but they do not flinch from it either. In every cold camp, they reinforce the core truth of the Wolf Scroll: that guardianship is not defined by ease, but by endurance. That the silent protector must be able to suffer without losing focus, to be cold without growing bitter, to be tired without becoming careless.

Endurance over comfort. Discipline over ease. Stillness over struggle. These are the laws of the cold camp—and they form the spine of the pack.

CHAPTER 6:

The Watch Turn – Rotations, Vigilance, and Faith

The night is not an enemy—it is a test. For the wolf-shinobi, the turning of the watch is not just a tactical necessity, but a sacred rhythm. It is where trust is proven without words, and where discipline lives not in grand acts of valor, but in quiet vigilance. While others sleep, one remains awake. And in that silent moment, the entire weight of the mission, the safety of the pack, and the continuation of the code rests on a single pair of eyes.

The watch turn is the pulse of the cold camp. It is the steady heartbeat that keeps chaos at bay, even in the deepest hours. The system is simple: time is divided, duty is shared, and vigilance rotates. But its simplicity masks its power. To take a turn at watch is to make a vow—to be the barrier between threat and rest, between night and survival. It is a rotation not just of labor, but of faith. Each shinobi trusts that the one before them held the line. Each shinobi ensures the next has something to inherit.

In many ways, the watch turn is the purest form of unspoken loyalty. No one watches the watcher. There are no inspections, no supervisors, no applause. Just the cold, the silence, and the commitment to stay awake for those who cannot. The one on watch does not have the luxury of drifting. Every creak in the trees, every rustle in the distance, every shift in the wind must be registered, cataloged, judged. Vigilance becomes not just a duty—but an identity.

To stand watch is to embrace stillness without passivity. The shinobi must remain alert, but not frantic; calm, but not dull. It is a balance between relaxation and readiness, between patience and immediate reaction. The greatest threat may never come—but the moment you stop expecting it, it arrives. The trained guardian scans not just with eyes, but with intuition. They feel the shape of the night. They listen to its changes. And they trust their instincts when something invisible begins to press against the edge of the perimeter.

But the watch turn is not just a personal burden. It is a communal contract. In a disciplined pack, everyone takes their shift without protest. The rotation is sacred. The chain must never be broken. When one falters—by sleeping through their shift, by losing focus, by allowing comfort to override duty—the chain fractures. And even if no harm results, the invisible bond that holds the group together weakens. Faith, once compromised, is difficult to restore.

This is why the shinobi trains not just for action, but for alertness. Watch shifts are practiced. Micro-naps are mastered. Nutrition is balanced with timing in mind. Even breathing is refined, conserving energy while sharpening attention. Some nights, the body screams for rest, and the cold tries to lull the senses. But the trained watcher knows that fatigue is a liar, and that survival is often determined in the moments when comfort would be easiest to surrender to.

Not all shifts are equal. The deepest hours—just before dawn, when the body is weakest and the cold is most biting—are the hardest to bear. And yet they are often the most dangerous, when enemies assume guards will be lowest in vigilance. For this reason, the pack rotates fairly. No one takes the easy hours every night. No one shoulders the worst alone. Even in hardship, there is balance. This is the structure that sustains trust without resentment.

There is also a quiet dignity to standing watch. The shinobi does not seek glory, but in those moments—standing between the sleeping pack and the unknown—there is a deep sense of purpose. You are not killing. You are not fleeing. You are simply holding the line. There is a clarity in that. A sacred kind of peace. Not peace as in comfort—but peace as in order. You are the keeper of that order.

There are nights when nothing happens. No threats arrive. No alarms are sounded. It is easy, then, for the undisciplined to question the need. To see the watch as wasted time. But the shinobi knows better. The absence of threat is not proof of safety—it is the result of readiness. Threats often choose the unprepared. And the presence of watch, night after night, signals to the world: *We are not prey. We are protected.*

Faith is what underpins the watch rotation. Faith that the one before you watched with equal care. Faith that the one after you will rise without delay. Faith that your sacrifice—though unseen—matters. This is not blind belief. It is earned trust, forged over countless nights of fulfilled duty. And when that faith is strong, the pack moves through even hostile terrain with a quiet confidence: someone is always watching. We are never fully vulnerable.

But faith is also tested. There will be nights when a member misses their rotation. When someone falls asleep on watch. When panic overrides judgment. These moments, while rare in a trained pack, must be handled with precision. Not with anger—but with correction. The failure is acknowledged, understood, addressed. And then the rhythm resumes. Because the most dangerous thing a pack can do is let failure fester. The rotation must continue. The trust must be rebuilt.

In cities, the watch may take different forms—surveillance cameras, electronic alerts, staggered foot patrols. But the principle remains unchanged: someone is awake while others rest. Someone is listening when the world is silent. Someone is standing, even when everyone else is down. The form may evolve, but the doctrine does not. Vigilance must be shared. Fatigue must be managed. And readiness must be constant.

To live by the Watch Turn is to embody faith in action. It is to believe in your comrades enough to stay awake when they need you most. And it is to trust that when your shift ends, someone will carry on what you began. This rhythm of sacrifice and trust, repeated night after night, becomes the quiet strength of the pack.

Because while anyone can fight, not everyone can wait.

And in the dark, it is the one who waits—who watches—who makes all the difference.

CHAPTER 7:

Rituals Beneath the Pines – Campfire Ethics

In the life of the nomadic shinobi, there are few constants. Terrain changes. Allies shift. Missions evolve. But beneath the pines, when the pack pauses long enough to exhale, there is a space—quiet, small, and sacred—where rituals are born. Not ceremonies of pomp or tradition, but simple, deliberate acts that keep the soul aligned. These are the campfire ethics: the invisible rules that govern behavior when the mission rests, the wind quiets, and warriors become human again for a brief moment.

The campfire is rarely lit. Flame draws attention. But the idea of the fire—gathering without walls, eating with discipline, sharing silence with intent—remains central. Beneath the pines, the shinobi observes an unwritten code. It governs not only how food is shared or gear maintained, but how dignity is preserved, how tensions are diffused, and how the line between solitude and solidarity is respectfully kept.

First among these ethics: **take only what you need**. In the wild, excess is betrayal. Every piece of meat, every swallow of water, every square of cloth carries weight. To take more than your share is to steal from someone else's endurance. But to quietly give more—passing your portion to someone wounded, sacrificing warmth for someone on edge—that is the mark of the guardian spirit. No one speaks of it. But everyone notices.

Second: **tend to your gear in silence**. Maintenance is meditation. After long treks, the pack gathers under the branches, each tending their blade, repacking their loadout, checking straps and knots. No one commands it—it just happens. The quiet hum of readiness. It's in these small rituals that a pack rebuilds its sharpness. A dull blade isn't just a liability—it's a reflection of the inner state. Discipline doesn't begin in the fight; it begins in the preparation.

Third: **no unnecessary talk**. Beneath the pines, silence is not a void—it's a space of respect. A shinobi speaks when there is something worth saying. A lesson. A warning. A shared memory offered as a gift, not a demand for attention. Conversation is low and intentional. Jokes, if shared, are brief and honest—never cruel. No one needs to prove themselves at the fire. That's what the terrain is for. Around camp, humility governs.

Fourth: **carry your weight without making it heavy for others**. Complaining is contagious. One voice of bitterness can sour a whole watch. A shinobi in the camp speaks of pain only when it becomes danger—an injury that must be addressed, a weakness that compromises the group. Otherwise, discomfort is carried like weather: endured without comment. The stronger help the weaker not by boasting, but by lifting more and speaking less.

Fifth: **respect solitude**. Not every warrior rests the same. Some speak little and watch the sky. Some sharpen tools for the fourth time, just to settle their breath. Others rest their heads on packs and pretend to sleep. The code beneath the pines allows for distance. There is no expectation of forced camaraderie. Presence is enough. Just knowing someone is near can be its own kind of strength.

Sixth: **settle disputes in whispers, not in front of the fire**. Conflict happens—minds fray in the cold, pride clashes in fatigue. But the camp is not the place for drama. Disagreements are pulled aside, handled with dignity, resolved without spectacle. A true shinobi does not perform righteousness. They seek restoration, not domination. Those who escalate around the fire reveal their lack of internal stillness. The mature solve problems in the shadows, and return to the light together.

Seventh: **honor the fallen, even in absence**. Every pack carries ghosts. Warriors lost in missions past. Names unspoken, memories folded into gestures. A ritual beneath the pines may be as simple as placing an extra bowl beside the fire, or wearing a piece of gear once belonging to a fallen brother. These acts are quiet reminders that no one truly walks alone—that every step taken now was bought by someone who can no longer walk.

Eighth: **leave the site cleaner than you found it**. The camp is not yours. It is borrowed from the earth. Whether a forest grove, a rooftop in an urban war zone, or the back of a broken supply truck—wherever the shinobi rests, they leave no rot, no trace, no arrogance. Crumbs are buried. Ashes scattered. Footprints brushed. The land owes the guardian nothing—and so, they take nothing. Even rest must be repaid with respect.

And finally: **look each other in the eyes before you sleep**. It's not spoken. But in every camp, there comes a brief glance—a nod between watchers, a look of unspoken trust between those about to rest and those rising for their shift. These moments are brief but binding. They say, "I've got you." They say, "You're not alone." For a life where words are few and risks are many, this simple exchange becomes the ritual of loyalty itself.

Campfire ethics are not taught in formal scrolls. They are absorbed through exposure, reinforced by observation, and honored in action. A new shinobi learns quickly what is expected, not because someone tells them, but because the weight of silence makes it clear. Break the code, and you are not scolded—but the pack shifts. Trust becomes cool. Distance grows. In this way, the ethics are self-enforcing. Not out of fear—but out of pride. No one wants to be the weak link. Everyone wants to be worthy of the fire, even if there is no flame.

When the pines sway above, and the mission has paused just long enough to breathe, it is the campfire ethics that keep the pack aligned. They are the rituals that restore without softening, that connect without clinging, that remind each warrior of who they are and why they serve.

And then, when the time comes to rise, the ground is brushed clean. The packs are hoisted. The circle breaks. And like wolves in mist, the guardians vanish into the next shadow— leaving behind nothing but peace.

CHAPTER 8:

The Sentient Perimeter – How to Feel a Threat Before It's Seen

Before the blade is drawn, before the alarm is sounded, before danger is named—there is a feeling. Subtle. Instinctual. A shift in wind. A pause in birdsong. A silence that shouldn't be there. The shinobi does not wait for confirmation from the eyes. They listen to what cannot be measured. This is the Sentient Perimeter—the unseen field around the pack where presence is felt before it is proven, where threat is sensed before it is seen.

A perimeter is not a line on a map or a ring of traps—it is a living awareness. In the doctrine of the nomadic guardian, the perimeter is not a fixed zone, but a fluid membrane of intuition, expanded and contracted based on terrain, weather, mood, and the presence of others. To treat it as static is to invite intrusion. A sentient perimeter breathes. It shifts with the wolves inside it. It adapts to context, and most of all, it listens.

A well-trained shinobi begins by listening to the land. The trees speak. The insects report. The birds signal. In a forest, silence is noise. When the usual sounds of life go quiet, something unnatural is moving. Predators make prey go still. Human presence—clumsy, unaware, out of sync—disturbs the subtle cadence of wilderness. The wolf-shinobi listens to this disturbance, not just with ears, but with skin. With gut. With breath.

In urban terrain, the language changes but the principle remains. A flicker of motion in a window where none should be. A car parked for too long with the engine still warm. A camera that blinks once. A bystander who doesn't act like a bystander. These are signals that the perimeter has been touched. Not broken, but brushed. A well-disciplined guardian feels these touches like a vibration in their ribs. They don't panic. They don't react loudly. They shift. They breathe deeper. They watch without staring.

The sentient perimeter begins inside the shinobi. Their body must be quiet enough to hear it. No anxiety in the breath. No erratic movement. No clouded emotion to fog the senses. A scattered mind produces a scattered field. Clarity sharpens the radius of awareness. In this way, the more grounded the warrior is in their own stillness, the further out they can feel. This is why cold camp discipline and watch rotation matter: they prepare the mind for this form of sensing.

There is also a spatial awareness that goes beyond the physical. A shinobi knows the energy signature of their pack.

They learn to feel who is where without looking. They know how each person steps, rests, shifts. So when something unfamiliar moves among them, it is noticed not because of sound, but because it doesn't belong to the known pattern. The body may not know why, but it knows it. A misstep. A wrong rhythm. The perimeter blinks. The wolf lifts its head.

The perimeter is never passive. It is tuned through habit. The pack moves with constant, subtle calibration: lines of sight established without speaking, fields of motion covered instinctively, unspoken roles taken as needed. It's not about setting traps or building walls—it's about becoming the trap. Becoming the wall. A perimeter lives in the eyes of the watchers, in the rotation of their presence, in the questions they ask the world just by how they breathe.

There are practical signs the shinobi reads, yes—footprints, disturbed leaves, displaced air, scent carried on wind—but those are confirmations. By the time the trail is found, the feeling has already arrived. The true mastery is not detection but pre-detection. Sensing the ripple before the rock is thrown. It is a muscle refined through countless hours of stillness and exposure, through failure and adjustment, through silence and survival.

When two or more trained shinobi hold a perimeter together, something deeper occurs. The field sharpens. Each one carries a portion of the awareness, like overlapping circles of vision. They do not need to speak to confirm a change. A glance is enough. A tilt of the head. A shift in breath. The network pulses with understanding. This is the invisible perimeter—not of sensors, but of shared trust. Of warriors so attuned to one another that they feel disruption at the same time.

There is an emotional dimension to this awareness as well. Fear is a signal. So is overconfidence. The perimeter reflects the energy of the pack. If one person is distracted, the whole field dulls. If one member is off balance, the threat slips closer. And so, the shinobi carries not only gear and blade— but emotional stillness. This is why ego is trimmed. Why inner conflict is managed. A perimeter can be breached from within just as easily as from without.

When the perimeter is touched—genuinely touched—the response is not noise. It is precision. A shift in stance. A hand on hilt. A signal passed without word. The shinobi does not chase shadows. They do not panic at every rustle. But when the shift is real, their body moves before conscious thought catches up. Because the training, the sensing, the mapping—

it's already done. The wolf doesn't wonder if the forest changed. It *knows*.

In environments where the threat is constant—war zones, occupied cities, decaying borders—the sentient perimeter must remain active even during movement. The pack walks in deliberate spacing, maintaining sight lines. Each turn of the head, each pause, is calculated. The front feels forward. The back listens behind. The middle monitors both. The formation breathes like a creature. And within it, each shinobi is both a node and a nerve ending.

Training this kind of awareness begins with humility. You must first admit that your body often lies to you. That comfort dulls instinct. That noise seduces the mind away from the field. You begin by stripping away excess. Then you expose yourself to the environment. You study how it behaves when left alone. You learn its moods. Its songs. Then, when something foreign enters it, the disharmony stands out.

The sentient perimeter is not a mystical gift. It is not a talent granted by birth. It is a skill built in silence, and paid for in hours of watchfulness. But once learned, it becomes one of the most powerful tools in the shinobi's kit—because it allows you to win the fight that never happens. To adjust before the danger arrives. To survive not by force, but by perception.

A threat seen is already halfway managed. A threat *felt*—before it ever appears—is often neutralized without a blade drawn. This is the art of the guardian wolf. To know without knowing. To feel without fear. To keep the pack safe before they even realize they were in danger.

This is not paranoia. This is presence.

And in the shadows, presence is everything.

忍びの術

CHAPTER 9:

Nonverbal Command – The Language of the Eyes

In the life of the shinobi wolf, words are rare. Not because they are feared, but because they are slow. Noise gives position. Speech invites interpretation. But the mission demands immediacy, clarity, and cohesion—even in complete silence. In the wild, wolves do not bark orders. They glance, they shift, they breathe with intent. Their leadership is felt before it is spoken. So too is the way of the nomadic guardian: command without volume. Direction without display. The language of the eyes.

Nonverbal command is not simply a matter of gestures. It is a doctrine built on mutual trust, pattern recognition, and emotional control. The pack does not need a map when every face carries a signal. The angle of the jaw, the twitch of a brow, the length of a stare—these are the lines of communication in the field. And they are sharper than any blade.

A shinobi's eyes must speak long before their mouth does. The pack learns this through constant observation—first by watching, then by mirroring. In training, the mentor does not shout. They fix the younger guardian with a look that says: *stand still, follow me, now is not the time*. These commands are absorbed through exposure. The student learns not to ask questions, but to read the air. They begin to recognize tension in the face as clearly as others read text. This is not mind-reading. This is attunement.

The foundation of this form of communication is presence. You cannot lead silently if your mind is scattered. The eyes give you away. Doubt has a weight. Hesitation leaves a trail. But when the shinobi carries clarity, it becomes contagious. A single look steadies the pack. The body speaks through stillness. The pupils speak through intensity. In the field, a commander's calm is louder than a speech. And that calm starts with the eyes.

There are many forms of this silent language. A narrow look and head tilt: *move left*. A slow blink: *wait*. A sharp cut of the eyes to the tree line: *threat, two o'clock*. A brief widening of the eyes: *ready weapons*. These signals do not exist in a manual. They are learned by operating in tight formation under pressure, again and again. Over time, the pack builds a shared vocabulary. Their own dialect of glances and nods. A system built on intuition and shared rhythm.

Importantly, these signals are not rigid. They shift with context. A glance that means *hold* during a patrol might mean *freeze* in an ambush. That is why the pack must move like a living organism—able to flex and interpret based on environment. The key to this fluid understanding is cohesion. A pack that trains together, suffers together, moves together—knows without needing to clarify.

This form of command is not about dominance. It is not about hierarchy enforced through threat or volume. It is influence without ego. The most effective leaders in the wolf scroll tradition are not those who bark the most orders—but those whose presence calms the storm. Their gaze carries weight because it is consistent. Reliable. Grounded in service, not in self.

The power of eye-based command also lies in how it honors the intelligence of the pack. It assumes every member is alert, present, and competent. There is no need to explain what everyone already senses. There is only the brief signal to act. This form of trust builds pride. Each member becomes more than a follower—they become a sensor, a strategist, a limb in the greater body of the unit.

In times of crisis, when visibility is poor or when tension frays nerves, it is the eyes that restore order. One look from the anchor of the pack can steady a panicked scout. One nod from the rear guard can green-light a movement. No raised voice needed. No chance of interception. These moments—fleeting as they may be—are the lifeblood of the silent warrior path.

This is why the shinobi must train their face as carefully as their body. A grimace at the wrong moment can transmit fear. A glance of doubt can unravel a plan. Discipline includes emotional mastery—not suppression, but regulation. The guardian learns to hold a neutral face even in chaos. Calm eyes even in grief. Focused eyes even in fatigue. Because every glance you give the pack is either fuel or friction.

Nonverbal command also honors terrain. In close quarters, noise bounces. In the woods, sound carries. In enemy territory, even a whisper can bring ruin. But eyes—if trained—speak with precision and without trace. The guardian does not need to lean close to communicate. They do not need to expose themselves to direct sound. They only need to be seen.

In rare moments, the eyes transmit something even deeper: intent. The pack may not know the full plan—but if the leader looks back with unwavering clarity, the pack follows.

Not because they understand every detail, but because they trust the direction. This is what makes nonverbal command so potent. It bypasses explanation and speaks straight to instinct.

There are, of course, limits. Nonverbal command fails if the bond is weak. If the team is unfamiliar, scattered, or ego-driven, silence becomes ambiguity. That's why cohesion must come first. Why rituals beneath the pines matter. Why the watch rotation builds faith. The pack that eats together, trains together, and endures together learns how to see each other. In those glances live a thousand unspoken affirmations: *I see you. I know what you need. Let's move.*

Technology may evolve. Radios may exist. Tactics may shift. But the ability to move as one without a single word will always be sacred. In the dark, where sound is danger and time is short, a single glance can carry a mission. A twitch of the eye can redirect fate. This is not drama—it is doctrine.

So train your gaze. Sharpen your awareness. Still your face until it becomes a mirror of your will. And when your moment comes, lead not with volume, but with vision.

The pack will follow.

Not because you told them to.

But because they saw.

CHAPTER 10:

Leading From Behind – Influence Without Ego

To lead is not to stand above. It is not to shout orders, demand obedience, or place oneself at the front of every charge. In the way of the shinobi wolf, leadership is not spotlight—it is shadow. It is not the loudest voice, but the quietest strength. The one who leads from behind does so without demanding recognition, without needing to be seen, without ever saying, *"I am in charge."* Because the pack already knows. The proof is in the stability of their movement. The cohesion of their choices. The calm in their center.

In nature, the alpha wolf does not always walk in front. It often lingers near the rear, watching the group's flow, adjusting pace without command. It does not interrupt unless it must. It trusts the pack to move in rhythm. And when that rhythm falters, it corrects with presence, not panic. This is the model of the nomadic guardian—leading without possessing, directing without dominating.

Leadership in the shinobi code is influence. But not the influence of charm or force—it is influence earned through clarity, consistency, and unshakable calm. It's not about being right; it's about being steady. Others look to you because your stillness allows them to find their own. In chaos, your breath remains even. In uncertainty, your eyes do not flinch. You are the one they orient around—not because you said to, but because their survival instinct recognizes something anchored.

This kind of leadership begins long before the mission. It is forged in training, in suffering shared without complaint, in countless small choices that show others who you are when no one is watching. You rise for your watch without being told. You take the worst seat near the cold. You give your ration to the wounded without ceremony. You listen when others speak but rarely speak to hear yourself. All of this builds a kind of gravity. And eventually, others begin to align themselves to your orbit.

To lead from behind is to allow others to step forward. It is to trust them to act, to risk, to fail and recover without stripping them of their autonomy. A true leader resists the urge to control. They guide subtly—like a hand on a shoulder rather than a leash on the neck. They watch the whole formation, adjusting from the rear. When someone shines, they step back. When someone falters, they step in. Not for credit—but for cohesion.

The ego cannot survive in this form of leadership. Ego wants credit, attention, status. But the shinobi leader operates in inverse: the greater their presence, the less they must show it. They give credit. They deflect attention. They measure success not by who notices their role, but by how well the mission continues without interruption. Their fingerprint is invisible—but it is everywhere.

The danger of conventional leadership is the hunger for centrality. To be the loudest voice. The most seen. The decision-maker. But in a pack built on mutual awareness, these impulses fracture unity. The louder the leader, the smaller the followers become. The more the leader needs to be right, the less room there is for collaboration. And eventually, the pack stops thinking. They wait to be told. They lose initiative. In the shinobi path, that is failure.

Instead, the leader from behind creates conditions for others to succeed. They recognize strengths and arrange them in formation. They remove friction before it's felt. They anticipate needs before they're spoken. And when things go wrong, they take responsibility—quietly, without shifting blame. Their influence isn't just tactical—it's spiritual. They make others feel stronger, braver, sharper—because their presence reminds others of their own power.

There is also a paradox here. The one who leads from behind must also be ready to step forward instantly when needed. When the structure collapses, when the forward scout is wounded, when confusion halts the flow—then the quiet leader moves. Not with noise, but with precision. Their authority is accepted immediately because it was already present. They don't have to assert it—it's simply recognized, like gravity. The pack falls in line not from fear, but from familiarity.

This kind of leadership also survives better in long campaigns. Commanders who lead from ego burn out or are isolated. But the quiet leader, embedded in the rhythm of the group, endures. Their style is sustainable. Their authority doesn't rely on volume, charisma, or hierarchy—it relies on trust, competence, and clarity. And those are renewable. They sharpen over time.

But to lead from behind does not mean weakness or indecision. It requires judgment. It requires moral strength. Because there will be moments when the pack veers. When the mood turns toxic. When poor decisions gain momentum. In these moments, the rear-positioned leader must intervene—not with domination, but with recalibration.

They do not shame. They redirect. Their correction feels like remembering, not reprimand.

To be this kind of leader, one must also lead oneself ruthlessly. You cannot ask others to be focused if you are not. You cannot inspire courage if you leak fear. The eyes are always watching—even if they pretend not to be. In the doctrine of the quiet leader, *you do not perform leadership. You practice it.* Every day. Through small actions, through restraint, through consistency. Your leadership is your breath. If it falters, so will the group.

When done well, this style of leadership leaves no signature. When the mission ends, the team may not even articulate why things felt smooth, why morale stayed high, why decisions were easy to make. But the leader will know. Because they didn't need to be in front. They just needed to be aligned. To be the quiet current under the surface. The one that carried everyone forward without resistance.

The world will always be filled with noise, with those who confuse control for leadership, presence for performance. But the wolves of the shinobi path know better. They follow the one who listens before they speak, who observes before they act, who lets others rise instead of stepping on them to climb.

And when the time comes to choose a path, when the team fractures under pressure, they'll look back—not for rescue, but for recalibration. And there you'll be.

Not to take over.

Just to remind them who they are.

And where they're going.

忍びの術

Samuel Franco

CHAPTER 11:

The Lone Watcher – Bearing the Weight When No One Sees

Every pack has its moment of sleep. Even wolves must close their eyes, even shinobi must rest. But someone must stay awake. Someone must watch the edges while others dream. Not for praise, not for status, not for acknowledgment—but because the mission demands it. The Lone Watcher is the one who carries the weight no one claps for. The one who bears the silence so others can heal. It is the most invisible role and often the most vital.

The Lone Watcher is not simply the one on duty during a night shift. This chapter is not about rotation or schedule. It is about *posture of soul*—a mindset of unshakable vigilance, practiced in solitude. This is the shinobi who sees the danger before it grows teeth. Who notices the tremor in a teammate's hand and says nothing but adjusts the loadout accordingly. Who stands at the edge of the firelight not because they were told to, but because someone has to.

To become the Lone Watcher is to step into the cold willingly. You won't be thanked for it. You won't be celebrated. Most will never know how many nights you kept still while your muscles ached, how many threats you tracked with your breath held, how many fears you buried so others could feel safe. That is the point. The Lone Watcher does not act for applause. They act for *continuity*. For the mission. For the pack.

This path requires more than stamina. It requires emotional durability—the ability to witness and carry the weight of danger, doubt, even despair, without transmitting it to others. While others collapse into exhaustion or fray in the face of uncertainty, the Watcher remains. Still. Anchored. Not because they feel nothing, but because they've trained themselves to *hold* what others cannot. They are the container of the unspoken.

There is a quiet loneliness to this path. You will feel it when everyone else sleeps. When the fire dies down and even the wind forgets to howl. In those hours, the Lone Watcher faces not just the external threat, but the inner shadows—the creeping thought that no one sees the burden you carry. That your effort is invisible. That maybe it doesn't matter.

But it does.

It matters in the way the pack breathes easier. In the way the silence remains unbroken. In the way danger seems to always arrive just after you shift the formation. The Lone

Watcher leaves no signature, but their presence is the difference between continuity and collapse. You are not there to be *seen*. You are there so others *don't have to see* what you guard against.

To walk this path well, you must understand your own mind intimately. Fatigue, resentment, boredom—these are enemies as dangerous as any intruder. You must learn to sit with them, let them pass, and stay sharp regardless. The Watcher does not allow distraction. They do not slip into fantasy. They are *here*—in this breath, in this second, in this shadow. Presence is not optional. It is the weapon.

You also must learn restraint. The Lone Watcher sees many things. Tension rising between teammates. Decisions made out of pride. Weakness concealed behind a brave face. You must decide what to act on and what to leave alone. You are not the commander. You are not the judge. You are the one who *notices*. And sometimes, noticing is enough. Sometimes, it is everything.

The Watcher also leads—but never in the usual sense. Their leadership is felt, not declared. They model discipline by embodying it. They create safety not by shouting orders, but by being the one who is always ready—always steady. The pack may not talk about it, but they feel it. They sleep more deeply when you're on watch. They check their weapons more carefully after watching how you clean yours. They mirror your seriousness when they realize you've never once let your guard drop.

This kind of leadership can't be taught in classrooms. It must be lived. Practiced. Failed at and returned to. Because there will be moments when the burden cracks your back. When you nod off and miss a signal. When you lose faith that any of it matters. What makes the Watcher is not perfection—but recovery. They return to the post. They correct. They remember their role. They endure.

And in doing so, they quietly become indispensable.

The Lone Watcher is not always physically alone. Sometimes, they walk beside others—but remain emotionally separate, because they are scanning when others are socializing. Sometimes, they move in groups—but are the only one carrying the full picture in their mind. Other times, they are *truly* alone—left behind to cover retreat, sent forward to scout silently, tasked with remaining awake during the most exposed moments. In every case, they carry the same essence: *watchfulness without recognition.*

To live this way long-term requires a strong internal compass. If you need constant approval, this role will crush you. But if you have made peace with solitude, if you draw strength from service rather than spotlight, the Lone Watcher becomes more than a role—it becomes an identity. A quiet honor. A silent oath.

There is also a sacred truth hidden here: that those who are seen the least often care the most. The guardian who stands at the edge of the group, weapon cradled, eyes always scanning—may seem distant, but is often the one who would bleed first for any of them. Their detachment is not apathy. It is protection. A necessary elevation from the noise of emotion so they can keep everyone alive.

The world will never reward you for being the Lone Watcher. But the pack will survive because of you. Missions will complete because of you. Lives will be lived because you were awake when it mattered. And though no one may ever say it aloud, every warrior who has rested under your watch will remember the feeling: that somewhere in the dark, someone was standing for them.

That someone was you.

Chapter 12:

Ghost Signals – Coordinated Movement Without Sound

In the world of the shinobi wolf, sound is a risk. Words travel. Echoes betray. A single whisper can collapse a mission. But movement must still happen. Direction must still be given. The pack must act as one, even when speaking is suicide. And so, there is another language. One older than words. One more precise than shouting. Ghost signals— silent cues, passed like wind, seen only by those trained to look for them.

These signals do not require devices or tools. They are not reliant on radios, lights, or codebooks. They are body memory, muscle rhythm, intuitive choreography. They are the nods, taps, shifts, and blinks that speak volumes without sound. They are invisible to outsiders but unmistakable within the pack. They are coordination without conversation.

To master ghost signals is to move like a shadow with many limbs. A single nod from the point shinobi means the rest change course. A hand paused in the air means halt. A slow circle of the index finger near the thigh means fan out. A closed fist held low? Prepare to engage. But these signals only mean what they mean because the pack has trained them into muscle. There is no magic—only discipline.

And subtlety.

Ghost signals must be *small*. Not exaggerated. Not theatrical. You do not wave arms like flags. You shift a foot. You draw a line in the dust with a boot. You let your shoulder tighten just slightly in the agreed direction. You allow your silhouette to be seen *only enough* by those who need to see it. The enemy must never know a message passed. That is the art. Command as ghost. Influence as flicker.

This level of coordination requires shared experience. A team that hasn't suffered together cannot ghost together. Each member must know the others' movement styles, blind spots, habits. They must know who needs a sharp gesture and who will respond to a breath. There is no one-size-fits-all. Ghost signaling is personal. It is refined in the field, under pressure, when the wrong twitch could mean the wrong move—and the wrong move could mean death.

Ghost signals are not just physical. They are energetic. A pause in motion can say "danger." A subtle delay in rotation timing can say "wait, something's wrong." Even the way someone breathes—or stops breathing—can transmit intent. Shinobi learn to feel these cues. They don't wait for confirmation. They *respond*. Like wolves adjusting in a hunt, each movement sets off a chain reaction.

But not everyone can lead this dance. The one who initiates ghost signals must be deeply attuned, not only to the mission, but to the people. They must move with confidence—not arrogance—and signal in a way that invites cohesion, not confusion. Their cues are clean, unhurried, unmistakable in their stillness. If a signal must be guessed, it has failed. The team must feel the message in their bones, not debate it in their minds.

This requires trust. A pack that does not trust will hesitate. And hesitation kills coordination. You must believe—without proof—that the hand sign you caught in the corner of your eye was intentional. That the signal to freeze came from a place of awareness, not panic. And you must *commit*. The pack that ghosts together moves like mist—dispersing and regathering with silent precision.

The power of ghost signals is most evident in environments where noise is fatal: deep woods under moonlight, cities during surveillance, enemy-held territory with thin walls and open cars. Here, spoken commands would get you killed. But a shoulder shift gets you in position. A three-fingered tap on a knee lets the next movement begin. A slow exhale signals the time has come. Not a word is said, but everything is heard.

Importantly, ghost signals are not used for everything. They are reserved for moments that demand unity without sound. For ordinary tasks, the pack moves on known rhythm, pre-agreed routes, time-synced formations. But when the unexpected arrives, when deviation becomes necessary, ghost signals activate. They are the pulse of adaptation. The link between autonomy and unity.

And sometimes, the most powerful signal... is no signal at all.

Stillness. Chosen, deliberate stillness. When the leader does not move. When the pack breathes and no one initiates. This is the clearest message: *we wait. We hold. Something is off.* In the world of ghost coordination, stillness is not inaction—it is command. And the pack must be trained to recognize when silence *is* the signal.

Training this doctrine requires repetition under pressure. Drills in near-darkness. Movement with blindfolds. Exercises where voices are banned, and mission success depends entirely on awareness. The pack must learn to feel each other through walls. To predict timing. To anticipate shifts. To *become fluent* in the silence between them.

New members struggle. They want confirmation. They crave explanation. But over time, if they are kept close and trusted deeply, they begin to adjust. They learn to quiet their bodies. To watch with intention. To move in sync, even without knowing all the why. This is how a pack expands—slowly, patiently, without dilution of discipline.

When ghost signals are mastered, the effect is eerie. From a distance, the team appears telepathic. No voice, yet all shift together. No signal seen, yet everyone moves. It seems like choreography. In truth, it is *trust performed at speed*. It is shared intuition shaped by experience. It is the doctrine of wordless unity, practiced until it becomes instinct.

To the outside world, it looks like magic.

To the shinobi, it is just another tool.

Another vow kept in silence.

Another bond that doesn't need proof.

Because in the Way of the Nomadic Guardian, the best communication is invisible. The strongest commands leave no echo. And the most disciplined warriors do not need to be told—they already know what to do when the wind shifts, when the hand drops, when the shoulders stiffen.

They move.

Together.

Like ghosts.

CHAPTER 13:

Adaptive Packs – How to Build Without Owning

The traditional world tells you to build by claiming. To make a place yours by fencing it. To earn loyalty by branding it. To forge a team by controlling it. But the shinobi wolf knows another way. One more suited to movement, to instability, to mission-driven bonds. The pack does not need walls to be strong. It does not need ownership to be real. It needs only *alignment*. And from that, an adaptive pack is born.

In the doctrine of the nomadic guardian, to "build without owning" means creating strength without possession. It means forming unity without clinging. The pack comes together not through contracts, but through shared hardship, discipline, and purpose. It remains flexible, evolving, and mobile—never tied to one form, one leader, or one location. Because when everything changes, the rigid shatter. But the adaptable endure.

The adaptive pack is forged by values, not by location or blood. Its members do not need matching insignia. They don't need the same accent, uniform, or history. What they share is the *Way*. The discipline of silence. The ethic of guardianship. The deep instinct to watch one another's blind spots, to respond with precision, and to keep moving. The adaptive pack can be assembled from anywhere—so long as the alignment is real.

To build this kind of unit, ego must be removed. You are not collecting followers. You are not building a kingdom. You are not the sun that others orbit. Instead, you are *part of the current.* Sometimes you lead. Sometimes you support. Sometimes you step out of the formation so it can evolve without you. You do not *own* the pack. You *serve* it—and in doing so, it grows stronger.

This demands a new kind of humility. You must let go of the desire for permanence. Adaptive packs shift by necessity. People move in and out. Some will walk with you for years. Others for hours. The bond does not weaken because of its duration. It is measured by presence, by action. The one who shares your fire for a single night but guards it with their life is as much your kin as any lifelong companion.

Ownership tries to freeze things. It says, "This is mine. This is how it must stay." But the path of the shinobi is seasonal. The terrain shifts. The threat evolves. The team must respond. Roles change. Leaders rotate. What mattered in one mission may be a liability in the next. You must be willing to let go of formation to preserve function. To dissolve one pack in order to form a better one.

This doesn't mean betrayal. It means clarity. When you build without owning, you honor what *is*, not what *was*. You do not hold onto a teammate whose heart has gone cold, nor do you resist the presence of a new one whose fire is aligned. You adapt—constantly, consciously. Because the mission requires it.

The strength of an adaptive pack lies in its modularity. It can shrink to two, swell to twenty, split and regroup. It does not rely on one structure. It has no sacred shape. What is sacred is *responsiveness*. Who covers what field of vision? Who carries the heavy load this time? Who steps forward when the previous leader falls silent? All of this is decided not by titles—but by need, by awareness, by trust earned in motion.

This trust is the backbone. And it must be rebuilt constantly. In adaptive packs, there is no "resting on history." You show up *again and again*. Each mission is new proof. Each campfire another layer of cohesion. And when trust is broken, it is addressed directly or cut clean. The pack cannot afford rot in its center. Adaptation requires honesty—swift, sharp, and grounded in care, not control.

Building without owning also means your knowledge, your tools, your methods—must be shared, not hoarded. In rigid hierarchies, power is stored in secrecy. In adaptive packs, it is distributed. Everyone knows how to lead. Everyone trains to cover every role. Not because they always will—but because resilience requires redundancy. The mission does not die if one wolf falls.

There is a particular kind of freedom in this approach. You do not fear being replaced—because you were never installed. You do not cling to your title—because your identity is in the *work*, not the role. You contribute, you evolve, and when needed, you step aside. The pack remains. That is legacy enough.

But freedom comes with responsibility. Without a central power to enforce order, the pack must be *self-policing*. Every member must uphold the ethic. Complacency is poison. Ego must be challenged. When someone forgets the way— whether through arrogance, apathy, or fear—they must be reminded. Not shamed, but recalibrated. Or, if needed, released.

Because the adaptive pack does not make space for dead weight.

And yet—it *always* makes space for the willing. If you arrive raw but sincere, if you move with humility and readiness, if you prove your intent through discipline—then you are part of it. Even without a past. Even without ceremony. The pack adapts. It stretches to include you. It does not ask for your resume. It asks for your readiness.

This is how movement becomes culture. How a shifting team becomes a lasting force. You may not control who stays or goes, but you control *how* you operate—how you train, how you respond, how you protect. That way, no matter who surrounds you, the form remains strong. Because you have practiced the principle, not just the performance.

And when the mission ends, when the pack dissolves again into distance and silence, you are left not with loss—but with gratitude. The bond was real, even if temporary. The structure was strong, even if invisible. The impact was lasting, even if nameless. You built something. You owned nothing. And yet, you left the terrain changed.

That is the Way.

Build. Adapt. Release. Continue.

Always forward. Always aligned.

CHAPTER 14:

The Refuge Principle – Safety You'll Never Be Thanked For

In the life of a shinobi wolf, safety is both a refuge and a responsibility. It is not a place, but a principle—a silent promise to those who rely on the pack's vigilance. The Refuge Principle teaches that true safety is often invisible and uncelebrated. It is the quiet work done behind the scenes, the barriers built without fanfare, the shelter offered without expectation of thanks.

This safety is not comfort. It is readiness. Not rest, but refuge. When the pack settles, it is not to ease but to fortify—to create a bastion in hostile terrain where vulnerability can be managed, not eliminated. The Refuge Principle recognizes that safety is not an absolute state, but a dynamic condition maintained through vigilance, discipline, and sacrifice.

The shinobi's refuge is a space where wounds can be tended, plans can be made, and spirits can be steadied. It is a momentary pause in the endless motion of survival. But this sanctuary is fragile. It exists only because some wolves remain awake while others dream. Because boundaries are watched even when no threat is visible. Because every corner is scanned and every silence tested.

The paradox of the Refuge Principle is that it asks its guardians to sacrifice visibility for security. Those who build safety rarely receive acknowledgment. Their efforts dissolve into routine, their presence taken for granted. The pack benefits from their work, but the credit is invisible. And yet, this invisibility is a badge of honor. To protect without recognition is the purest form of loyalty.

Creating refuge requires more than physical barriers. It demands mental and emotional containment. The refuge must be a space where anxiety can be held safely, where fear can be acknowledged without panic, where trust can be rebuilt if fractured. The guardian of the refuge holds these invisible boundaries as tightly as any wall or watchtower.

This principle extends beyond the campfire circle. It applies to every environment—urban shadows, wilderness, the spaces between. The Refuge Principle means knowing when to engage, when to withdraw, and how to create pockets of safety amid chaos. It means being the calm eye in the storm, steady and unyielding.

Safety also means preparation. The shinobi understands that refuge is not found by chance. It is built by design—by choosing terrain carefully, by establishing watch rotations, by minimizing exposure. Each detail, no matter how small, contributes to the whole. A disturbed twig, a misplaced campfire, an unguarded trail can undo hours of work. The refuge is only as strong as its weakest link.

Guardians who embody the Refuge Principle understand the weight of responsibility. They know that a single lapse can endanger the entire pack. They accept that their vigilance may cause discomfort or frustration. They do not seek gratitude, only the knowledge that their duty protects lives.

In living this principle, the shinobi practices humility and patience. The refuge is not a fortress for glory, but a haven for survival. It is a reminder that sometimes the greatest strength lies in the spaces we create for others to endure. The Refuge Principle teaches that loyalty is often shown in the quietest acts—watching, waiting, defending what cannot be seen.

To honor this principle is to recognize the unseen labor that holds the pack together. It is to trust those who build safety without applause. It is to understand that in the shadows of the night, the true guardians stand watch, creating refuge for the living—without ever asking to be seen.

CHAPTER 15:

The Returnless Scout – Giving Without Recognition

In the silent tapestry of the shinobi's path, the returnless scout walks a unique and solemn thread. This is the warrior who moves forward, offering their eyes and ears to the pack without expectation of praise, without promise of return. Their gift is the rawest form of service: to give completely, knowing their name will fade into shadow, their deeds may never be spoken, their sacrifices unseen. To be the returnless scout is to embody a profound humility and devotion that transcends ego and recognition.

The returnless scout does not march to the sound of drums or heralds. They slip through the terrain like a ghost, bearing witness to threats and opportunities alike, returning not with glory, but with the weight of knowledge. Sometimes, the scout never returns at all—absorbed by mission, by fate, by sacrifice. Their absence is part of the silent calculus the pack accepts. Their gift is not their presence, but the absence they leave behind, which sharpens the pack's awareness and resolve.

The role of the scout is ancient, predating armies and empires. It is the vital act of gathering intelligence, mapping danger, and creating space for others to act. Yet, in the shinobi's world, this task demands more than skill; it demands a surrender of self. The returnless scout must move beyond personal survival, beyond desire for accolade, and into a state of total commitment to the mission and the pack's survival.

To walk this path is to understand that giving without recognition is an act of faith—faith in the pack, in the mission, in the Way. The scout trusts that their unseen work will ripple outward, protecting lives they may never meet, shaping victories they will never claim. This faith must be unwavering because the path is lonely. Scouts move on edges—physical, emotional, spiritual—carrying burdens in silence, bearing the weight of solitude.

The loneliness is not a void but a crucible. In solitude, the scout hones patience and clarity, sharpening senses to a razor's edge. They learn to listen to the wind, to watch the shadows, to read the subtle signs that escape others. The returnless scout is a master of anticipation, navigating terrain and threat with a quiet confidence born from experience and trust in instinct.

But this path is perilous. Scouts often face the choice between revealing themselves to warn the pack and remaining hidden to survive. Sometimes, they must sacrifice their own safety to ensure others' survival. This tension defines the returnless scout's existence. They do not seek martyrdom but accept that sacrifice is an intrinsic part of their role.

Within the pack, the returnless scout's contribution is both invisible and invaluable. Without their eyes on the frontiers, the pack would stumble blindly into danger. Their silent vigilance allows the rest to move with purpose and assurance. The scout's absence is often felt as a presence—a space filled with unspoken knowledge and unwavering loyalty.

Training for this role is rigorous. It demands physical endurance, mental resilience, and emotional fortitude. Scouts learn to master concealment, navigation, and survival in isolation. They cultivate mindfulness, controlling fear and loneliness, maintaining focus over long hours and uncertain outcomes. Above all, they cultivate a spirit that finds meaning not in recognition, but in the quiet impact of their giving.

The returnless scout's greatest gift is trust—the trust that their work, unseen and unsung, is the foundation of the pack's strength. This trust sustains them through darkness and doubt. It reminds them that their path, though solitary, is never without purpose.

To embody the returnless scout is to give fully and without condition. It is to accept the silence that follows sacrifice. It is to move forward when others turn back. It is to hold the mission above self. And in doing so, the returnless scout becomes a living testament to the deepest loyalty of the shinobi—the loyalty that demands no thanks, only action.

忍びの術

Samuel Franco

CHAPTER 16:

Death for the Living – The Quietest Form of Protection

In the shadowed way of the shinobi wolf, death is not the end but a tool wielded with the utmost restraint and purpose. It is the quietest form of protection, an ultimate act of sacrifice carried out in silence for the sake of the living. This is the doctrine that recognizes death as a guardian's last vow—a shield forged from finality, guarding those who carry on.

To embrace this truth is to confront the most profound paradox of the shinobi path: that sometimes, survival depends on the willingness to die. But not for glory, nor for revenge, nor for recognition. Death in this doctrine is a gift offered selflessly—a final wall that absorbs the storm so the pack may endure. It is the deepest form of loyalty, where the individual's end becomes the beginning of protection for others.

The shinobi understands that death is not to be sought recklessly. It is not a performance or a burden to flaunt. It is a last resort, held in readiness, respected as a sacred boundary. Those who carry the willingness to die do so with calm clarity, knowing their sacrifice is the quiet foundation of safety and continuity. It is a power held in stillness.

This principle shapes the way the shinobi live daily. The acceptance of death tempers fear and sharpens focus. It informs every decision—from how the pack moves through hostile terrain, to when and where conflict is engaged, to how each guardian positions themselves to shield others. The shadow of death is ever present, yet it is not a specter of despair, but a steadying force that demands discipline and honor.

Death for the living also means embracing invisibility in sacrifice. The shinobi who gives their life does so without expectation of ceremony or remembrance. Their passing is often unrecorded, unnoticed beyond the small circle of kin who bear the loss quietly. This invisibility is part of the protection. To expose such sacrifice risks unraveling the fragile safety the pack has built.

The protector's death is therefore a guarded secret, a final act of silence. The wolf who falls absorbs the threat, halts the danger, and passes on the path for others. In this act, death is transformed from a defeat into a deliberate strategy—a last defense that buys time and space. It is the wolf's final howl, muffled by snow and shadow, echoing only in the hearts of the living.

This form of protection demands a particular mindset. It requires acceptance of one's limits and an understanding of the larger whole. The shinobi does not act as a lone hero but as a part of the pack's lifeblood. Death becomes a currency, spent with solemn care for the survival of many. To live without this readiness is to carry a weakness that can fracture the pack's integrity in moments of crisis.

Training for this path is rigorous. It is not enough to prepare the body and sharpen skills; one must also cultivate mental resilience to face mortality without fear or hesitation. Meditation on impermanence, ritual discipline, and the constant reinforcement of purpose are the armor that girds the shinobi. The warrior who truly embraces death's quiet protection moves without hesitation, acts with precision, and yields only when the mission is complete or the pack is safe.

The Doctrine of Death for the Living also extends beyond the battlefield. It teaches that protecting others is not limited to combat but includes enduring hardship, absorbing blame, and bearing burdens that others cannot. Sometimes, it means becoming the shield against despair, the unseen support that carries the weight of others' pain. This too is a form of sacrifice—a living death that preserves life.

Within the pack, this understanding creates a sacred trust. Each member knows that their comrades carry this readiness—not as a threat, but as a promise. It creates a bond that transcends words: the knowledge that someone will stand between you and oblivion, even if it costs them everything. This knowledge fortifies courage and strengthens resolve.

In the end, death for the living is the quietest vow a shinobi can make. It is the last thread holding the pack's fabric together when all else unravels. It is a sacrifice unseen but deeply felt. It is a lesson in humility, loyalty, and the profound power of selflessness.

To walk this path is to accept the ultimate cost in order to safeguard the future. It is to become the silent guardian of life's fragile flame, willing to extinguish one spark to ensure the blaze endures.

CHAPTER 17:

The Packless Phase – Surviving Isolation Without Losing Heart

In the life of the shinobi wolf, the pack is a source of strength, safety, and purpose. But there are times— inevitable times—when the pack fractures, when the familiar circle dissolves, and the wolf stands alone. This is the Packless Phase: a period marked by isolation, uncertainty, and profound challenge. To survive this phase without losing heart is to confront the deepest tests of resilience and identity, and to emerge tempered rather than broken

Isolation is often seen as a punishment or a failure. But within the doctrine of the shinobi, it is also a passage. The packless phase is not the end of kinship, but a crucial space for reflection, renewal, and self-reliance. It is where the wolf learns to stand on its own claws before the next pack forms, where endurance is forged in solitude rather than numbers.

The first challenge in the packless phase is the silence. Without the hum of kinship, the wolf faces the echoes of its own thoughts and fears. Loneliness can become a gnawing predator, threatening to consume clarity and will. Yet silence is also a teacher. It reveals weaknesses, exposes hidden strengths, and offers the space to rebuild the internal compass. To survive isolation, the shinobi must learn to listen—to the world, to the body, and to the quiet voice within.

Without the pack, there is no shared purpose to bind action. The wolf must cultivate a new mission, often intangible and deeply personal. This mission might be survival itself, preparation for reunion, or simply maintaining the Way through discipline. Whatever the focus, it must be unwavering. A drifting wolf is lost. Purpose anchors the spirit, giving direction to movement and thought.

Physical endurance is vital. The packless phase tests the limits of body and mind. Without support, the wolf faces hardship alone—harsh weather, scarce resources, and constant vigilance. These conditions sharpen resilience but also threaten despair. Maintaining discipline over diet, rest, and training becomes a lifeline. Each small victory—keeping warm, moving silently, finding food—reaffirms control and sustains hope.

Mental resilience is equally crucial. The absence of communal reassurance demands an internal reservoir of strength. The shinobi must learn to manage doubt and fear without external comfort. Practices such as meditation, visualization, and ritual become tools to maintain focus and sanity. The wolf trains the mind as rigorously as the body, building a fortress of calm amid chaos.

Emotionally, the packless phase is a crucible. The pain of separation, the sting of loss, and the weight of solitude test the heart's endurance. Yet, the shinobi does not deny these feelings but accepts them as part of the journey. To survive without losing heart is to hold grief and hope in balance, to carry sorrow without letting it consume the will to continue.

The doctrine teaches that connection does not vanish in isolation. The wolf remains linked to the pack through memory, loyalty, and shared values. This invisible bond sustains identity and purpose. The shinobi draws strength from the thought of reunion, from the knowledge that the pack exists even when apart. This faith in kinship beyond presence is a lifeline.

Adaptability is a key survival skill in this phase. The wolf must adjust to solitude, to new terrain, and to unpredictable conditions. Flexibility in tactics and mindset prevents stagnation. The packless shinobi learns to become a singular pack, merging all roles within itself—leader, scout, guard, healer—balancing these identities with care.

Importantly, the packless phase is not permanent. It is a transition, a liminal space between chapters of kinship. The shinobi remains open to new alliances, new formations. Rejoining or rebuilding a pack requires discernment—trust rebuilt slowly, ego set aside, and roles redefined. The wolf who has endured alone returns tempered, aware of both the strength and fragility of connection.

Within this phase lies an opportunity for profound growth. The wolf gains a clearer understanding of self—its fears, strengths, and purpose—unfiltered by group dynamics. It sharpens autonomy without sacrificing loyalty. It embraces solitude as a tool rather than a punishment.

The packless phase also teaches humility. Without the collective identity, the shinobi confronts the rawness of individual existence. This confrontation strips away illusions of invincibility, grounding the warrior in reality. From this humility springs wisdom—an awareness that strength lies not just in numbers but in the integrity of one's spirit.

Ultimately, surviving the packless phase without losing heart means embracing paradox. The wolf is alone yet connected. Vulnerable yet strong. Lost yet purposeful. This balance is the essence of the shinobi Way—an enduring dance between movement and stillness, presence and absence, solitude and kinship.

The packless phase tests the shinobi's loyalty to the Way itself. Can one remain true when all external bonds are severed? The answer is found in persistence, in discipline, and in faith. Faith in the path, faith in self, and faith that the pack is never truly gone.

As the phase wanes and new kin emerge, the wolf carries forward the lessons of isolation. The scars and strengths borne alone become threads woven into the fabric of the new pack. The experience deepens empathy, sharpens awareness, and fosters a deeper commitment to guardianship.

In this way, the packless phase is not a void but a crucible— an essential rite of passage that tempers the shinobi's heart and spirit. To survive it without losing heart is to prepare for the next chapter of loyalty, territory, and guardianship with renewed clarity and strength.

The shinobi who endures isolation becomes not only a survivor but a bearer of wisdom—a wolf who has faced the wilderness of solitude and returned to the pack whole, ready to lead, to follow, and to protect once more.

Chapter 18:

Burden of Loyalty – When Kinship Endangers the Mission

Loyalty is the lifeblood of the shinobi pack. It is the thread that weaves individuals into a cohesive whole, binding warriors with shared purpose, trust, and sacrifice. Yet loyalty is not without its shadows. There comes a time when the very kinship that sustains the pack can become its heaviest burden—when loyalty threatens to blind, to divide, and to endanger the mission itself. Understanding and navigating this peril is a test of both character and leadership.

The burden of loyalty emerges most sharply when personal ties and collective duty conflict. The shinobi, bound by invisible chains of kinship, faces a wrenching choice: uphold the pack's integrity or protect a comrade whose actions may jeopardize the greater goal. This tension is a crucible for discipline, demanding clarity above affection, justice above comfort, and purpose above all.

Loyalty, by its nature, is often unconditional—a sacred vow to stand by one another through adversity. But within the Way of the shinobi, loyalty must also be conditional upon the mission's success and the survival of the many. Blind loyalty is a trap. It allows the pack to fracture from within, sows distrust, and compromises operational effectiveness. The burden is knowing when loyalty becomes a liability.

The doctrine teaches that true loyalty is not servitude but stewardship. It is the responsibility to protect the pack's vision, even when it requires difficult decisions. Sometimes, this means confronting a kin who errs, holds back, or endangers others. These moments require courage— speaking truth in the face of resistance, enforcing discipline without alienation, and balancing mercy with necessity.

When loyalty endangers the mission, the shinobi must remember the larger purpose. The pack is greater than any one member, and the mission transcends individual bonds. Protecting kin at the cost of the mission is a betrayal of all. It undermines trust, weakens unity, and places the entire group at risk. The burden lies in weighing compassion against consequence, in choosing what serves the collective good.

This tension can fracture the pack's spirit. Some wolves may cling to loyalty as a shield against loss, unwilling to see faults or risks in their kin. Others may prioritize the mission coldly, dismissing bonds and eroding morale. Both extremes threaten balance. The shinobi's path demands a middle way—a loyalty tempered by discernment, humility, and a commitment to truth.

Leadership plays a pivotal role in carrying this burden. Leaders must model the courage to face uncomfortable realities and to act in the pack's best interest, even at personal cost. They cultivate an environment where loyalty includes accountability, where kinship does not excuse failure, and where difficult conversations are a mark of strength, not weakness.

The burden also weighs on the individual. Each shinobi must navigate their own loyalties—to comrades, to the mission, to personal values. This internal conflict can be isolating and painful. The Way encourages reflection and meditation to reconcile these tensions, fostering a mindset where loyalty is an active choice, not a blind chain.

In practice, the burden of loyalty manifests in many ways. It may require stepping aside a beloved comrade whose judgment falters. It might mean delivering hard truths that fracture relationships but preserve integrity. It often demands sacrifice—prioritizing the mission over personal feelings, even when it wounds the heart.

The shinobi understands that carrying this burden is part of guardianship. Loyalty is not merely a comfort but a responsibility—a responsibility that includes difficult decisions made in the silence of the soul. To evade this burden is to betray the very essence of kinship.

Yet, this principle does not condone callousness. True loyalty recognizes the humanity of every wolf and seeks to restore, redeem, and rebuild whenever possible. Discipline is balanced with compassion, and consequences with opportunities for growth. The aim is not punishment but preservation—of the pack, the mission, and the Way.

The burden of loyalty also shapes how the pack evolves. It forces constant evaluation and adaptation, preventing stagnation and decay. Through honest reckoning, the pack becomes stronger—more resilient and united by tested bonds rather than blind allegiance.

In the end, the burden of loyalty is a quiet test of character. It asks each wolf: How far will you go for your kin? What will you sacrifice to protect the mission? How do you balance love and duty when they seem at odds? The answers define not only the shinobi's path but the survival of the pack itself.

To carry this burden is to embrace the paradox of loyalty—a force that both binds and challenges, that comforts and confronts. It is the weight borne by those who choose to guard not only with weapons but with wisdom, and who understand that sometimes, true loyalty means making the hardest choices in silence and solitude.

CHAPTER 19:

When the Pack Fractures – Leadership in Frayed Brotherhood

Every pack, no matter how strong or loyal, faces moments of fracture. These breaks—whether born from conflict, loss, betrayal, or external pressures—test the resilience of kinship and the resolve of leadership. When the pack fractures, the bonds that once held tight may loosen, threatening chaos and disarray. Leadership in such moments becomes both the sharpest challenge and the most critical necessity. It demands a delicate balance of strength and empathy, decisiveness and patience, vision and humility.

Fractures in the pack can manifest in many ways: simmering resentments, breakdowns in communication, fractured trust, or outright division. These cracks threaten the very foundation of the shinobi's way, for the pack's power lies in unity, discipline, and shared purpose. When unity falters, so too does the ability to guard, endure, and prevail.

Leadership during this frayed phase is not about forceful control or blind command. It requires an acute awareness of the emotional and practical fissures within the group. The leader must first acknowledge the fracture—denial only deepens the divide. By recognizing and naming the tensions, the leader invites openness and begins the work of healing.

In moments of fracture, communication becomes paramount. The leader must foster dialogue, creating a space where grievances can be voiced without fear of retribution, where wounds are acknowledged rather than ignored. This openness can be uncomfortable, even dangerous, as it risks exposing vulnerabilities and cracks. Yet it is essential for rebuilding trust and understanding.

The leader must also embody patience. Healing a fractured pack is not a swift task. It requires time for reflection, for processing pain, and for reestablishing bonds. The leader walks alongside the wolves, showing steadfastness without rushing resolution. They understand that some fractures may never fully heal, but that the pack can still function with honesty and respect.

A crucial aspect of leadership in this phase is the balance between individual needs and collective goals. Wolves may feel isolated or betrayed, craving personal recognition or justice. The leader must honor these feelings while steering focus back to the mission and the greater good. This requires diplomacy and sometimes difficult decisions—prioritizing what serves the pack's survival over individual desires.

The fractured pack tests leadership's capacity for humility. The leader must be willing to admit mistakes, accept criticism, and adjust course. Authority without humility breeds resentment and fracture; leadership that listens and adapts can mend divisions and strengthen bonds.

Moreover, the leader's example of integrity and consistency becomes a beacon in uncertain times. Wolves look to their leader not just for orders but for reassurance and hope. The leader's steadiness under pressure reaffirms the pack's identity and purpose, even as cracks threaten cohesion.

Leadership in fractured brotherhood also demands vigilance against further erosion. The leader must guard against factions, gossip, and divisive behaviors, addressing them swiftly and fairly. They reinforce the values that bind the pack—loyalty, discipline, sacrifice—and remind the group of their shared path.

At times, leadership requires making hard choices—removing disruptive elements, resetting roles, or even accepting losses. These actions are never taken lightly but may be necessary to preserve the whole. Such decisions are made with the pack's future foremost in mind, grounded in a commitment to the Way rather than personal power.

Importantly, the leader fosters resilience. They remind the pack that fracture is not the end but an opportunity to grow stronger through adversity. Lessons learned in brokenness build wisdom, deepen trust, and forge a more adaptable group. The pack that endures fracture is not perfect, but it is real and ready.

In this way, leadership during fracture becomes a test of spirit as much as skill. It requires a deep understanding of human nature—its flaws and potential—and a steady commitment to nurturing both. The leader becomes the guardian of the pack's soul, tending wounds while guiding forward.

The frayed phase also challenges the leader's ability to sustain personal resilience. Bearing the weight of division, managing conflicts, and making difficult decisions can isolate the leader. They must cultivate their own support—through mentors, ritual, or quiet reflection—to remain effective and grounded.

Ultimately, leadership in a fractured pack is a profound act of service. It is the willingness to hold the tension between discord and unity, to carry the pain of division, and to shepherd the wolves back toward connection and purpose. It is the embodiment of the shinobi's quiet strength—a force that does not dominate but nurtures, that does not command but inspires.

When the pack fractures, the Way of the shinobi does not call for the leader to conquer the breach with force, but to heal it with wisdom, courage, and heart. Through this leadership, the pack may not return to what it once was—but it can become something stronger, more resilient, and more deeply bound by the trials it has survived.

CHAPTER 20:

The Doctrine of Distance – Protecting Without Closeness

In the life of the shinobi wolf, protection is often imagined as an act of closeness—standing side by side with one's kin, shoulder to shoulder against danger. Yet, the Doctrine of Distance teaches a more subtle, and often more difficult, form of guardianship: protecting without closeness. This principle acknowledges that sometimes the safest and most effective defense requires maintaining distance—emotional, physical, or tactical—while still upholding unwavering vigilance and loyalty.

The Doctrine of Distance arises from the reality that proximity is not always synonymous with protection. In some circumstances, being too close exposes both the guardian and those they protect to greater risk. The shinobi must learn to read these situations with clarity and restraint, balancing intimacy with necessary separation. This is not detachment borne of apathy but a deliberate discipline, a calculated guardianship exercised from the margins.

Physically, distance in protection can mean maintaining space between kin and threat, adopting strategic positions that maximize safety and observation rather than immediate contact. It requires mastery of perimeter defense, understanding terrain, and anticipating danger before it reaches the inner circle. The shinobi moves like a shadow on the edge, the silent boundary that keeps the pack safe without crowding or exposing it.

Emotionally, the Doctrine of Distance is even more complex. It teaches that sometimes the warrior must guard the heart as much as the body. Over-attachment or unchecked emotions can cloud judgment, breed vulnerability, and lead to rash decisions. The shinobi learns to cultivate a controlled empathy—a fierce loyalty that does not dissolve into dependency or compromise. This emotional distance protects not only the individual but the integrity of the pack.

The challenge is maintaining connection without losing oneself in closeness. The shinobi must be present, attentive, and caring, yet hold boundaries that preserve clarity of purpose. This balance prevents the corrosive effects of codependence, jealousy, or favoritism, which can fracture the pack from within. Distance here is a form of respect—a recognition that each wolf carries responsibility for their own path while remaining part of the whole.

Tactically, the Doctrine of Distance is vital in modern and urban contexts, where traditional proximity is impractical or dangerous. Wolves within walls, for example, must adapt pack tactics to environments where direct contact with kin or threats is limited. Surveillance, remote coordination, and layered defense become tools to protect without physical closeness. The shinobi becomes a guardian of zones rather than points, a sentinel watching from afar while ready to strike when necessary.

This doctrine also fosters resilience. When the wolf understands that protection is not always about immediate rescue or presence, they develop patience and long-term thinking. They learn to trust in systems, rotations, and indirect safeguards. This shift requires humility—accepting that control is partial and that distance does not mean neglect.

Distance as protection also involves sacrifice. The shinobi may choose to withhold involvement or step back from immediate crises to preserve greater safety. This restraint can be misunderstood as abandonment, but it is a calculated decision rooted in the commitment to the pack's survival over momentary impulses.

The Doctrine of Distance is further reflected in the way information is shared within the pack. Sensitive knowledge is compartmentalized to minimize risk, with wolves entrusted only what they need to fulfill their roles. This selective sharing is a form of protection that balances transparency with caution, maintaining operational security without severing trust.

Moreover, distance nurtures self-reliance. Each wolf, while part of the pack, must be capable of independent action and decision-making. This autonomy prevents overdependence and ensures that the pack remains functional even when fragmented or dispersed. Protecting without closeness means trusting kin to carry their weight, supporting rather than smothering.

Spiritually, the doctrine is a meditation on impermanence and boundaries. It acknowledges that all relationships are transient, that proximity may ebb and flow, and that the shinobi's role is to guard the Way regardless of physical or emotional distance. This perspective fosters equanimity—a calm acceptance that guards against despair when distance is forced by circumstance.

Practicing the Doctrine of Distance demands rigorous discipline. The shinobi trains not only in physical endurance and tactical skill but also in emotional regulation and situational awareness. It requires constant vigilance—not just against external threats but against internal impulses that erode boundaries or cloud judgment.

Ultimately, protecting without closeness is an expression of profound trust. It trusts in the pack's cohesion beyond immediate presence, in the unseen connections that hold the group together through space and silence. It trusts in the strength of individual wolves to stand guard on their own, knowing that the whole remains guarded through their collective effort.

The Doctrine of Distance reminds the shinobi that guardianship is not always visible or tangible. It is often a quiet watchfulness, a measured restraint, and a faith in the unseen bonds of loyalty. Through this doctrine, the wolf learns that protection is as much about space and boundary as it is about action and proximity.

In embracing this doctrine, the shinobi becomes a guardian not only of bodies but of balance—between connection and separation, presence and absence, closeness and distance. It is a subtle, often lonely path, but one that ensures the pack's survival in times and places where proximity is a liability, not a safeguard.

Through the Doctrine of Distance, the shinobi cultivates a protective spirit that endures beyond touch and sight, a vigilance that bridges the gaps between wolves and holds the pack secure across the vast and shifting terrain of life.

忍びの術

Samuel Franco

Chapter 21:

Wolves Within Walls – Applying Shinobi Pack Tactics to Urban Life

The ancient lessons of the shinobi and the wolf pack—loyalty, vigilance, discipline, and kinship—were forged in the wilds, in forests, mountains, and open terrain. Yet as the world evolves, the challenges facing the modern shinobi demand adaptation. The urban environment, with its concrete walls, labyrinthine streets, and dense populations, presents a different kind of battlefield. Here, the doctrine of the pack must be applied within confined spaces and shifting social landscapes. The wolf pack becomes "Wolves Within Walls," adapting their tactics to survive and thrive amidst the complexities of city life.

Urban life compresses space, multiplies variables, and obscures threats beneath layers of noise and distraction. The traditional pack's open terrain tactics—surveillance, communication, perimeter defense—must be reimagined for the crowded, vertical, and often unpredictable urban environment. This requires the shinobi to develop new skills, new strategies, and new understandings of territory and trust.

One fundamental shift is the understanding of territory itself. In the wild, territory is often clearly defined by natural boundaries—rivers, ridges, or dense forest. In the city, territory becomes fluid and layered: a block, a building, a network of streets, or even an invisible digital landscape. The pack must learn to navigate these shifting boundaries, claiming and defending spaces in ways that balance visibility and secrecy.

Communication within the urban pack changes as well. The loud calls and signals of the wild are replaced by subtle gestures, coded language, and technology-assisted coordination. Silence remains a virtue; noise is a liability. Wolves within walls develop a keen sensitivity to nonverbal cues—eye contact, body language, light patterns, and even digital signals—to maintain cohesion without attracting unwanted attention.

The dense population of the city introduces new dynamics of trust. While the forest pack relies heavily on kinship bonds and long-term relationships, urban wolves often form temporary alliances, coalitions of convenience, and adaptive packs that shift according to circumstance. This requires flexibility in choosing whom to trust, a sharpened instinct for reading intentions, and a willingness to adapt quickly as alliances form and dissolve.

Security and defense in urban settings demand an emphasis on layered protection. The pack learns to guard multiple perimeters—from the front door to inner sanctums—using surveillance cameras, electronic monitoring, and controlled acccss points. Movement through city spaces requires stealth and precision; every step can reveal or conceal. The shinobi moves with the calculated grace of the wolf stalking prey, mindful of shadows and lines of sight.

Urban life also demands a heightened awareness of the social environment. Wolves within walls must navigate complex human dynamics—neighbors, authorities, rival groups—and understand how social influence and perception shape safety and power. The pack's strength lies not only in physical readiness but in social intelligence, negotiation, and the ability to blend into the background.

The doctrine of adaptability becomes crucial. Urban packs are less permanent and more fluid than their forest counterparts. Wolves may shift roles, change locations, or alter tactics quickly in response to new threats or opportunities. This flexibility prevents stagnation and keeps the pack resilient amid the city's constant flux.

Training within walls involves a blend of old and new—traditional martial arts, weapons skills, and stealth tactics combined with modern technology, surveillance methods, and digital security. Wolves learn to use smartphones, encrypted communication apps, and electronic countermeasures as tools of the trade, merging ancient discipline with contemporary innovation.

Leadership in urban packs requires a nuanced approach. The leader must be a strategist, a diplomat, and a guardian of morale. They balance the need for secrecy with the necessity of transparency within the group. They foster trust in an environment where suspicion can easily take root and ensure that every member understands their role in the intricate social and physical networks of the city.

Perhaps the greatest challenge of wolves within walls is maintaining the pack's spirit amid isolation and alienation. Urban life can be isolating, with individuals separated by walls, screens, and social barriers. The shinobi pack must work intentionally to preserve connection, rituals, and shared purpose, ensuring that the urban environment does not erode the bonds that give strength.

At its core, the transformation from forest pack to urban pack is a testament to the shinobi's enduring principle: adaptability. The wolf's spirit is not confined to any one landscape. Whether beneath towering pines or towering skyscrapers, the values of loyalty, discipline, and guardianship remain constant. The tactics evolve, but the Way endures.

Wolves within walls remind us that the essence of the pack is less about geography and more about connection—how individuals align purpose, communicate trust, and move as one. The city, with all its challenges, becomes just another terrain to master, a new proving ground for the ancient art of the shinobi.

In mastering urban pack tactics, the shinobi embrace a new frontier, one that demands intelligence, subtlety, and an unwavering commitment to the Way. The wolf's howl may be silent in the city streets, but its presence is felt—watchful, resilient, and ready to protect the pack from shadows both seen and unseen.

CHAPTER 22:

Long Winter Readiness – Psyche of Prolonged Operation

The wolf's survival depends not only on physical strength and tactical skill but on an unyielding mental fortitude— especially during the long winters, those extended periods of hardship and scarcity when endurance is tested to its limits. The concept of Long Winter Readiness in the shinobi pack is a meditation on psychological resilience, preparation, and the mindset necessary to sustain prolonged operations in isolation, adversity, and uncertainty.

In nature, winter is a season of dormancy and survival. Food is scarce, days are short, and the cold is relentless. For the shinobi, the "long winter" represents any prolonged challenge—missions extending beyond easy endurance, times when physical comfort is sacrificed, sleep is sparse, and threats persist beyond the momentary. It is a test of spirit as much as body, where mental stamina becomes the defining factor in success or failure.

Preparation for long winters begins well before the season arrives. It is a discipline of foresight—stockpiling not only supplies but also psychological resources. The shinobi trains the mind to anticipate hardship, to remain calm in the face of uncertainty, and to embrace discomfort as a path to growth rather than a punishment. This mental training is as crucial as physical conditioning, for the mind is both the battleground and the sanctuary during prolonged operation.

A critical aspect of Long Winter Readiness is the cultivation of patience. The shinobi learns to accept that progress may be slow or invisible. When days blend into nights, and fatigue clouds vision, it is patience that sustains forward momentum. Impatience breeds mistakes and fractures the resolve; patience fosters endurance and clarity.

Another cornerstone is adaptability. The long winter demands flexibility in tactics and mindset. Plans must be fluid, capable of shifting as conditions change. The shinobi embraces uncertainty, viewing it not as a threat but as an opportunity to innovate and overcome. This adaptability includes managing scarce resources wisely, improvising shelter and sustenance, and adjusting schedules to conserve energy and maximize efficiency.

Isolation is an inevitable aspect of prolonged operation. Long winters often mean long stretches without contact, companionship, or reassurance. The shinobi confronts solitude head-on, cultivating internal dialogue and mental rituals that maintain connection to purpose and pack.

Practices such as meditation, visualization, and journaling become tools to anchor the mind, prevent despair, and reinforce the mission's meaning.

The psyche of prolonged operation also requires vigilance against mental fatigue and burnout. The shinobi is trained to recognize signs of emotional depletion—frustration, hopelessness, distraction—and to employ strategies to counter them. These might include deliberate rest cycles, small rituals of self-care, or mental reframing techniques that transform suffering into strength.

Leadership during long winters plays a pivotal role. Leaders must maintain morale, enforce discipline, and foster a sense of shared purpose even when tangible progress is scarce. They serve as the emotional anchors of the pack, embodying resilience and reminding others of the greater mission beyond immediate discomfort.

The long winter is also a time for deep reflection and internal growth. Stripped of distractions, the shinobi confronts fears, doubts, and weaknesses. This confrontation is painful but necessary; it purges illusions and strengthens character. The mind that endures the long winter emerges sharper, wiser, and more prepared for future trials.

Preparation for long winters includes building routines that impose structure amid uncertainty. Consistent rituals— whether physical training, gear maintenance, or mental exercises—provide stability and a sense of control. These routines create a rhythm that counters chaos and anchors the shinobi's identity.

Nutrition and physical care remain vital, even when resources are limited. The shinobi learns to optimize minimal sustenance, to manage injuries silently, and to listen attentively to the body's signals. Long winter readiness means balancing exertion with conservation, knowing when to push forward and when to retreat into recovery.

The social dimension of long winters, though often reduced, is not neglected. When possible, maintaining connection with the pack—even if only through sparse communication or shared rituals—bolsters mental endurance. The awareness that one is part of something greater, that others are enduring alongside, fuels perseverance.

The doctrine of endurance over comfort is never more evident than in the long winter. The shinobi embraces hardship not as an enemy but as a teacher. The cold, the hunger, the isolation—all become crucibles that forge strength, discipline, and clarity. The wolf's howl may be silent in these times, but its spirit is loud and persistent.

Long Winter Readiness also calls for humility. The shinobi accepts that not all battles will be won quickly, and that survival itself is often the greatest victory. This humility tempers ambition and nurtures wisdom, reminding the pack that endurance is a marathon, not a sprint.

Ultimately, the psyche of prolonged operation is a testament to the wolf's unyielding spirit. It is the quiet determination that holds through darkness, the inner fire that refuses to be extinguished by cold or time. Long Winter Readiness is not merely surviving the harsh season—it is thriving within it, growing stronger and more capable with each passing day.

The shinobi who masters this doctrine carries the knowledge that no winter lasts forever, but the strength built within it endures across all seasons. This strength, born of patience, adaptability, and mental resilience, becomes the foundation upon which the entire pack's survival rests.

CHAPTER 23:

When the Alpha is Silent – How to Lead Without Direction

In every pack, the presence of the alpha—strong, decisive, and visible—often symbolizes the heartbeat of leadership. But what happens when the alpha falls silent? When direction is absent, and the traditional signals of guidance are muted or missing? This chapter explores the difficult, yet crucial, role of leading without clear direction, a challenge faced by shinobi and wolves alike in moments of crisis, uncertainty, or loss.

The silence of the alpha is not always literal. Sometimes it manifests as indecision, absence, or withdrawal—a leadership vacuum that threatens to unravel the cohesion of the pack. This silence can be disorienting; wolves accustomed to clear commands and decisive actions find themselves adrift. The instinct to follow falters when the path is unclear, and chaos threatens the pack's survival.

Leading without direction requires a profound shift in mindset and approach. It demands that those who step forward to fill the void do so not by asserting control, but by fostering adaptability, trust, and collective resilience. It is a leadership born of service rather than authority, a guidance that emerges through listening, observation, and quiet influence rather than loud commands.

One of the first lessons in this form of leadership is the recognition that direction is not a fixed point but a fluid process. When the alpha is silent, the pack must navigate ambiguity together, relying on shared values, past experiences, and mutual trust. Leaders in these moments become facilitators, helping the group to coalesce around common purpose and emergent consensus rather than dictating a predetermined course.

This style of leadership also emphasizes empowerment. Without clear direction from above, every member of the pack must take responsibility for their role and decisions. The leader encourages initiative and autonomy, trusting the wisdom and skills of the wolves around them. This distributed leadership strengthens the pack's resilience by harnessing collective intelligence rather than depending on a single voice.

Emotional intelligence is critical in this context. When uncertainty reigns, fear and frustration can easily spread. The leader's role becomes one of emotional steadiness, modeling calm and confidence even in the absence of clear answers.

This calm steadies the pack, preventing panic and maintaining focus on immediate priorities.

Communication shifts from top-down commands to horizontal dialogue. The leader facilitates open, honest exchanges, ensuring that concerns, ideas, and observations circulate freely. This openness not only generates creative solutions but also reinforces trust, a vital currency when formal authority is weakened.

The leader must also be comfortable with ambiguity and impermanence. In the absence of clear direction, decisions may need to be tentative, subject to revision as new information emerges. This requires humility—a willingness to admit uncertainty and adapt course as needed. The shinobi who masters this form of leadership understands that rigidity can be fatal, while flexibility fosters survival.

A critical tool in leading without direction is cultivating a shared mental model—a common understanding of the situation, the stakes, and the pack's core mission. This shared mental framework acts as a compass when explicit orders are lacking, guiding decisions and actions through collective alignment on fundamental principles.

Leading without direction often means embracing paradox. The leader must be both present and unobtrusive, guiding without dominating. They must balance confidence with openness, strength with vulnerability. This nuanced presence creates a space where the pack can self-organize and thrive despite uncertainty.

Training and preparation play an important role in readiness for such leadership. The shinobi pack that practices autonomy, cross-training, and shared decision-making is better equipped to navigate the alpha's silence. The culture of the pack—its rituals, values, and communication patterns—becomes the backbone that supports decentralized leadership in crisis.

The absence of the alpha also invites reflection on the nature of leadership itself. Leadership is not a role held by a single individual but a dynamic function that flows through the pack as circumstances demand. Sometimes leadership emerges from unexpected quarters—quiet observers, skilled scouts, or even those traditionally seen as followers. Recognizing and valuing this fluidity prevents stagnation and empowers the entire pack.

In urban or modern contexts, where hierarchical structures may be less rigid, the ability to lead without direction is especially relevant. Teams often face complex, rapidly changing environments where no clear roadmap exists. The shinobi's lessons on decentralized, adaptive leadership offer a timeless guide for navigating such uncertainty.

At its core, leading without direction is an act of faith—faith in the pack, in shared values, and in the collective strength of the wolves. It requires courage to step into the unknown, to trust others, and to embrace the messy process of emergent order. This courage is not born of ego but of commitment to the pack's survival and growth.

Ultimately, the silence of the alpha can become a powerful catalyst for transformation. It challenges the pack to grow beyond dependence on a single leader, to develop resilience through shared responsibility, and to deepen trust through collective navigation of uncertainty. In this way, the absence of direction reveals the true strength of the pack—not in hierarchy, but in unity.

The shinobi who understands how to lead without direction carries forward the ancient wisdom of the wolf pack, embodying a leadership that is both humble and powerful, silent and commanding. This leadership ensures that even in silence, the pack moves forward, protected and connected, through the shifting shadows of the unknown.

忍びの術

CHAPTER 24:

Legacy Without Insignia – The Tracks You Leave Behind

In the world of the shinobi and the wolf pack, legacy is not marked by trophies, titles, or public accolades. It is silent, subtle, and often unrecognized —etched instead in the invisible trails left behind, in the lives shaped, the missions completed, and the quiet influence that ripples far beyond immediate sight. The shinobi's legacy is a path traced not by insignia or grand monuments, but by the tracks they leave in the snow: faint, enduring, and meaningful only to those who know how to read them.

Legacy without insignia speaks to the essence of humility in the way of the shinobi. The greatest warriors do not seek glory or recognition. They move like shadows, their deeds known only to those they protect and those who come after. Their impact is measured in survival, in the preservation of knowledge and values, and in the strength of the pack that carries their spirit forward.

This form of legacy emphasizes the importance of actions over words. It is the small decisions, the unseen sacrifices, the moments of steadfast loyalty and quiet courage that create a lasting imprint. These tracks may not be celebrated or recorded in histories, but they form the foundation upon which future generations build.

One key element of legacy without insignia is mentorship. The shinobi understands that their influence extends through the teaching and shaping of others. Passing down skills, wisdom, and values ensures that the pack endures beyond the individual. This transfer of knowledge is not boastful or grandiose; it is practical, deliberate, and rooted in trust.

The concept also highlights the impermanence of physical marks and the endurance of intangible influence. Buildings crumble, scrolls decay, and even memories fade, but the character and resilience instilled in others persist. A shinobi's true legacy lies in the hearts and minds of those who continue the path, embody the doctrine, and adapt it to new challenges.

Legacy without insignia requires a keen awareness of one's impact on the environment and community. The tracks left behind must be sustainable and respectful—protecting the territory, preserving balance, and nurturing the ecosystem of relationships. Reckless actions, even if hidden, can harm the pack's future and sever the delicate web of trust and loyalty.

This principle also teaches the power of subtlety. The shinobi's influence often works through indirect means—shaping outcomes without direct confrontation, guiding decisions without overt control, and inspiring without visible leadership. The most profound legacies are sometimes those that go unnoticed at the moment but reveal their significance over time.

Another dimension of legacy is the acceptance of anonymity. The shinobi embraces the reality that their name may never be known, their face never seen. This anonymity is not a loss but a gift, freeing them from ego and enabling true selflessness. It allows their work to serve a greater purpose without distraction or desire for credit.

The legacy left by the shinobi also extends to the intangible values they embody—loyalty, endurance, adaptability, and silent guardianship. These values become the unwritten code that guides the pack and influences future paths. The shinobi's tracks are the lessons carried in stories, practices, and the shared memory of the pack.

In modern terms, legacy without insignia challenges the culture of visibility and recognition. It reminds us that meaningful impact often occurs behind the scenes, in quiet service and unseen sacrifice. It calls on leaders and warriors alike to focus not on personal fame but on the enduring strength of the collective.

Reflection on legacy also inspires mindfulness in the present moment. Every action contributes to the path that others will follow. The shinobi moves deliberately, aware that their tracks may guide those who come after through shadowed forests or uncertain terrain.

Ultimately, legacy without insignia is the deepest expression of the shinobi's way—a testament to the power of humility, perseverance, and the invisible bonds that hold a pack together across time. It honors those who lead, protect, and sacrifice without fanfare, leaving behind a trail that, though unseen by many, is unmistakably clear to those who understand the language of the wolf.

As the sun sets on the shinobi's journey, it is not medals or monuments that endure but the silent tracks in the snow— enduring marks of a life lived in loyalty, courage, and quiet guardianship. These are the true legacies, the paths that light the way for those who walk after, carrying forward the eternal spirit of the wolf pack.

APPENDICES:

Appendix A:
The Wolf Scroll Code — Key Principles Summarized

This appendix offers a concise summary of the core principles and doctrines detailed throughout *The Wolf Scroll of the Shinobi*. Use this as a quick reference or a daily reminder of the values and tactics that form the backbone of the shinobi pack.

- **Loyalty Beyond Words:** Trust is earned in silence and proven through consistent action.
- **Territory as Responsibility:** Defend what the pack relies on, even if it's not "owned."
- **The Nomad Code:** Belong without attachment; movement and flexibility are survival.
- **Endurance Over Comfort:** Discipline means choosing resilience, especially in hardship.
- **Silent Leadership:** Influence often comes from serving quietly, not dominating loudly.
- **Nonverbal Communication:** The eyes and subtle gestures speak louder than words.
- **Adaptive Packs:** Build bonds based on necessity and trust, not ownership or possession.
- **The Refuge Principle:** Protect others discreetly, without expectation of thanks.
- **Legacy Without Insignia:** Leave behind influence through actions, not recognition.

Appendix B:
Glossary of Wolf Pack Terms

Understanding the unique language and symbolism used in *The Wolf Scroll* strengthens comprehension and practice. Below are key terms and their definitions:

- **Alpha:** The leader or primary guide of the pack.
- **Packless Phase:** Periods of isolation when a shinobi operates alone, sustaining self-reliance.
- **The Quiet Fang:** The unspoken oath of loyalty and vigilance.
- **Ghost Signals:** Methods of silent communication during covert operations.
- **Refuge Principle:** The ethic of providing unseen protection and sanctuary.
- **Nonverbal Command:** Communication through eye contact and subtle body language.
- **Doctrine of Distance:** Maintaining protection without emotional or physical closeness.
- **Long Winter Readiness:** Mental and physical preparedness for extended hardship.

Appendix C:
Practical Exercises for Shinobi Training

These exercises help cultivate the mental and physical disciplines essential to the shinobi way:

- **Silent Vigil Practice:** Spend thirty minutes each day observing a space without moving or speaking. Focus on detecting small changes and threats.

- **Nonverbal Communication Drills:** Pair with a partner to practice conveying complex messages using only eye contact and hand gestures.

- **Endurance Conditioning:** Simulate "cold camp discipline" by training in challenging weather or environments, prioritizing patience and control over speed.

- **Rotational Watch Training:** Create a schedule for rotating vigilance duties within a group, emphasizing trust and alertness.

- **Mental Resilience Meditation:** Develop mindfulness sessions focusing on accepting discomfort and uncertainty without resistance.

Appendix D:
Ethical Considerations and the Shinobi's Code

A reflection on the moral framework guiding shinobi actions:

- The shinobi respects life and territory, avoiding unnecessary harm.
- Loyalty to the pack and mission never excuses betrayal of personal honor.
- The quiet guardian balances secrecy with responsibility toward community welfare.
- Protecting others often requires sacrifice, undertaken without desire for recognition.
- Leadership is service, not domination.
- Adaptability must never become opportunism at the expense of integrity.

. ABOUT THE AUTHOR:

 Samuel Franco is a dedicated practitioner of shinobi no jutsu, originally from Peru, who now resides in Lima Ohio. With years of experience in martial arts, Franco has developed a deep appreciation for the spiritual teachings of Shinobi no jutsu, which he believes are crucial in today's world. As a professional interpreter and translator, Franco brings a unique perspective to his work, blending linguistic skills with his martial arts expertise to bridge cultures and traditions.

In addition to his career, Franco is a part-time author and martial arts instructor, passionate about sharing the true essence of shinobi no jutsu. He strives to reconnect modern practitioners with the ancient, spiritual teachings of this art, emphasizing its principles of discipline, strategy, and personal growth. Franco's commitment to preserving and transmitting the authentic wisdom of the shinobi continues to inspire his students and readers alike.

The Shinobi Scroll of the Wolf
Loyalty, Territory, and the Way of the Nomadic Guardian

In the silent shadows where trust is forged without words, the wolf pack endures—bound not by chains but by loyalty, resilience, and an unbreakable code. *The Shinobi Scroll of the Wolf* reveals the ancient doctrine of the nomadic guardian: how to defend what isn't yours, lead without ego, and survive in solitude.

Blending timeless wisdom with practical strategy, this scroll teaches the art of quiet guardianship. From mastering the language of the eyes to navigating fractured brotherhoods, from enduring harsh winters to leaving a legacy without insignia, it guides you through the unseen paths of the shinobi wolf—adaptable, silent, and fiercely loyal.

For those who seek strength in stillness, leadership without dominance, and kinship beyond blood, *The Shinobi Scroll of the Wolf* is a map for walking the hidden trails of endurance and honor. Step into the shadows and discover the tracks left by those who protect in silence.

The wolf does not announce its loyalty. It shows it.

Made in the USA
Monee, IL
23 July 2025

21727721R00095